While every precaution has been taken in the preparation of this book, the publisher assumes no responsability for errors or omissions, or for damages resulting from the use of the information contained here in.

AI MADE SIMPLE: A SHORT BUSINESS GUIDE
First edition, December 2024
Written by Alex Hartem
Copyright © 2025 Hartem Writers

ALEX HARTEM

AI Made Simple:

A SHORT Business Guide

Essential AI Tools and Tips
with Intelligent Solutions for
Small Businesses and Entrepreneurs

HARTEM
WRITERS
INDEPENDENT PUBLISHING HOUSE

Content

THE TECHNOLOGICAL TRANSFORMATION OF MODERN BUSINESSES 7
- Overview of Artificial Intelligence in Everyday Applications 8
- Real-world Applications 9
- Unveiling Machine Learning 11
- Understanding APIs 14
- Automation: Streamlining Processes 15
- Chatbots: Revolutionizing Customer Interaction 19
- Practical AI integration: Food & Service 22

INTEGRATING AI INTO YOUR BUSINESS: A STRATEGIC GUIDE 24
- Steps to Implement AI Successfully 26
- Measuring the Impact of AI on Your Business 29
- Leveraging AI for Process Optimization 31

UNLOCKING AI'S BUSINESS POTENTIAL 33
- Boosting Efficiency with Automation 34
- Predicting Trends with Data Insights 36
- Personalizing Customer Experiences 38

CRAFTING YOUR AI GAME PLAN 40
- Why AI is the Next Big Step for Your Business 41
- Setting Clear Objectives: Defining Your AI Vision 41
- Building a Strong Data Foundation 43
- Leveraging Cost-Effective AI Solutions 45
- Empowering Your Team with AI Knowledge 47
- Seamlessly Integrating AI into Business Processes 48

DIVING IN CONTENT CREATION WITH AI 51
- Transforming Content Strategies with AI Solutions 54
- Be aware of AI in content creation 56
- Integrating AI in content creation 58
- Content Personalization and Audience Engagement 62
- Measuring Impact 64

ENSURING THE TRUSTWORTHINESS OF AI SOLUTIONS 67
- Testing is Crucial 70
- Safeguarding Data and compliance 74

- Data Protection in AI Applications 82
- Ethical Navigation in the Age of AI 83

WORKPLACE DYNAMICS AND AI 86

- The employer's perspective 87
- The employee point of view 90
- Human Skills and AI Capabilities 92
- Preparing for the Future of Work 93

TOOLS TO USE NOW 96

Chapter 1

The Technological Transformation of Modern Businesses

In the current era, technology plays a pivotal role in every industry, fundamentally reshaping how businesses operate and interact with their customers. The rapid evolution of technology, particularly in areas such as automation and artificial intelligence, has led to significant transformations in job roles and responsibilities across the globe.

Automation, which involves the use of technology to perform tasks with minimal human intervention, has streamlined processes, increased efficiency, and reduced operational costs. Industries ranging from manufacturing to services have adopted automated systems to enhance productivity and accuracy. For instance, in manufacturing, robots are now commonly used for assembly lines, while in the service sector, automated systems handle customer inquiries and transactions.

Artificial intelligence, on the other hand, encompasses a wide range of technologies that enable machines to mimic human cognitive functions. This includes learning, reasoning, problem-solving, and understanding natural language. AI has found applications in various fields, such as healthcare, where it assists in diagnosing diseases, and finance, where it helps in fraud detection and risk assessment. The integration of AI into business operations not only improves decision-making but also enhances customer experience through personalized services.

Additionally, application programming interfaces (APIs) have become crucial in the technology landscape, allowing different software applications to communicate and share data seamlessly. APIs enable businesses to integrate various services and platforms, fostering innovation and collaboration. For example, a retail company can use

APIs to connect its e-commerce platform with payment gateways, inventory management systems, and customer relationship management tools, creating a cohesive and efficient operational framework.

Chatbots, powered by AI, represent another significant advancement in technology. These virtual assistants can engage with customers in real time, providing support and information around the clock. By automating customer service interactions, chatbots not only enhance user experience but also free up human agents to focus on more complex issues. This shift towards automated customer engagement is transforming how businesses manage customer relationships and support.

Overview of Artificial Intelligence in Everyday Applications

Artificial intelligence is often highlighted in the media for its capabilities to generate amusing images, voices, and other forms of entertainment. However, beyond these playful uses, AI holds significant potential in automating tasks and completing activities that may otherwise require extensive skills, time, or financial resources.

This chapter delves into the functional applications of AI, offering insights into how it operates, effective ways to craft prompts, available AI tools, and various practical use cases.

It refers to the simulation of human intelligence processes by machines, especially computer systems. This technology aims to create systems that can perform tasks that typically require human intelligence. AI encompasses various functions such as learning, reasoning, problem-solving, perception, and language understanding.

At its core, AI involves machines programmed to mimic human cognitive functions. This includes the ability to learn from experience, adapt to new inputs, and perform tasks that would normally require human intelligence. The goal is to create systems that can operate autonomously and make decisions based on data.

Real-world Applications

AI has a wide range of applications across different industries, demonstrating its versatility and effectiveness. Some notable applications include:

- **Language Translation:** AI-powered tools can translate text and speech in real-time, breaking down language barriers and facilitating communication across cultures. This technology is used in applications like Google Translate and various language learning platforms.

- **Healthcare:** Machine learning models assist in faster and more accurate patient diagnoses. For instance, AI algorithms can analyze medical images to detect anomalies, aiding radiologists in identifying conditions like tumors or fractures.

- **Video Content Adaptation:** AI can analyze video content to automatically generate subtitles, translate dialogues, or even adapt the content for different audiences, enhancing accessibility and engagement.

- **Fraud Detection in Banking:** AI systems utilize pattern recognition to identify unusual transactions and flag potential fraud. By analyzing vast amounts of transaction data, these systems can detect anomalies that may indicate fraudulent activity, helping to protect consumers and financial institutions.

- **Computer Vision:** AI technologies are employed in computer vision to identify objects, faces, and scenes in images and videos. This capability is used in various applications, including security surveillance, autonomous vehicles, and medical imaging.

- **Content Creation:** Tools like ChatGPT can draft tailored cover letters or generate creative content swiftly. This capability allows businesses to produce marketing materials and communications more efficiently.

- **Design:** AI-powered design tools expedite the visualization of concepts by generating realistic images. Designers can use these tools to create mockups and prototypes quickly, streamlining the design process.

- **Customer Feedback Analysis:** AI can analyze customer sentiments and feedback to identify improvement areas. By processing large volumes of feedback data, businesses can gain insights into customer preferences and pain points, informing their strategies.

It is important to consider that training and operating datasets and AI models can incur substantial costs due to the high computing power required.

While simpler models can be trained with less computing power, third-party AI tools often come with usage costs that should be considered when selecting a model. Organizations must weigh the potential return on investment against the operational costs associated with deploying AI solutions.

Overall, AI is a rapidly evolving field with the potential to transform numerous aspects of daily life and industry practices, making processes more efficient and enhancing decision-making capabilities.

Unveiling Machine Learning

Machine learning, a prominent subset of artificial intelligence, encompasses a range of algorithms designed to enhance their performance automatically through experience.

This process is fundamentally reliant on the availability of large volumes of data, which the algorithms utilize to make predictions or decisions without the need for explicit programming for each individual task.

AI, contrary to its portrayal in films, is fundamentally about creating systems that can mimic human intelligence through data-driven learning processes. Unlike humans who can learn complex tasks like driving relatively quickly due to prior experiences, computers must be trained on vast amounts of data to perform similar tasks. This training enables them to develop predictive models based on input data, a process known as machine learning.

At its core, machine learning revolves around predictive modeling, which involves analyzing large datasets to identify patterns and relationships. This allows the model to make informed predictions about new, unseen data based on the insights gained from the training data.

A practical illustration of machine learning in action is the training of a model using a vast collection of images. For instance, a model can be trained with thousands of images of various objects, such as cars, to enable it to recognize and classify these objects accurately in new images. This process typically involves techniques such as convolutional neural networks (CNNs), which are particularly effective for image recognition tasks.

The process of training AI models involves utilizing vast datasets to predict outcomes based on inputs. This training allows the models to learn patterns and make informed decisions.

To engage with AI effectively, it is important to understand its key components:

- **Generative AI:** Refers to systems trained on existing data to create new outputs, such as generating images or text based on patterns it has learned. It produces creative content based on prior data training.

- **Large Language Models (LLMs):** A subset of generative AI focused on written language, trained on vast amounts of text from sources like books and the internet. These models mimic human language but may also produce inaccuracies or "hallucinations" (fabricated information).

- **Hallucinations in AI:** Occur when AI generates content that appears accurate but is factually incorrect or nonexistent. Users must critically evaluate outputs to avoid misinformation.

Despite its potential, machine learning faces several challenges, one of the most significant being the collection of extensive and varied datasets necessary for effective training. High-quality, diverse datasets are crucial for ensuring that the model can generalize well to new data and perform accurately across different scenarios.

Additionally, issues such as data privacy, bias in training data, and the need for computational resources can complicate the implementation of machine learning solutions.

Overall, while machine learning offers powerful tools for automation and decision-making, it requires careful consideration of data quality and ethical implications to achieve optimal results.

AI Tools and Effective Prompts

The quality of output from generative AI models heavily depends on the clarity and detail of the input prompts. For instance, a simple prompt such as "generate a song" may yield a basic result, whereas a more detailed prompt like "create a romantic song about a breakup with sticky notes and lyrics" will produce a significantly enhanced output. This principle underscores the importance of precision in prompt formulation. The more specific and descriptive the prompt, the better the AI can understand the user's intent and generate a relevant response. This aspect is crucial for users looking to maximize the effectiveness of AI tools in their projects.

Popular AI Tools and Their Applications

Several AI tools are currently available (2024), each offering unique functionalities:

- **ChatGPT:** Known for enabling conversational interactions with AI, it can perform various text-based tasks such as drafting recipes or cover letters. Recent updates also allow for image generation, expanding its utility in creative fields every day.

- **AWS Party Rock:** This tool facilitates the creation of generative AI applications using natural language, simplifying processes like designing themed greeting cards based on user descriptions. It empowers users to create personalized content without needing extensive technical knowledge.

- **MidJourney and Dall-e:** Utilized for generating AI-driven images and videos, it is popular for its ability to create visually appealing content. Artists and marketers often use it to produce high-quality visuals quickly.

- **Notion AI**: Integrated within Notion, this tool leverages existing document content to generate contextually relevant outputs. It enhances productivity by streamlining the content creation process within the Notion workspace.

Understanding APIs

Application Programming Interfaces (APIs) are essential tools that facilitate communication between different software applications, allowing them to interact and share data seamlessly.

APIs serve as intermediaries that enable various systems to work together, regardless of their underlying technologies or programming languages. This capability is crucial in today's digital landscape, where businesses rely on multiple software solutions to operate efficiently.

To illustrate the function of APIs, consider the analogy of a waiter in a restaurant. Just as a waiter takes orders from customers and conveys them to the kitchen, APIs take requests from one application and relay them to another, ensuring that the right information is delivered and processed. This process allows for a smooth flow of data, much like how a waiter ensures that food is served promptly and accurately.

The importance of APIs in business cannot be overstated. They are vital for creating interconnected systems that enhance operational efficiency. By enabling different applications to communicate, APIs help organizations streamline their processes, reduce redundancy, and improve overall productivity.

For instance, a company might use APIs to integrate its customer relationship management (CRM) system with its marketing automation tools, allowing for better data sharing and more effective marketing campaigns.

Moreover, APIs play a significant role in fostering innovation. They allow developers to build new applications and services on top of existing platforms, creating opportunities for new business models and revenue streams. This flexibility is particularly important in a rapidly changing technological environment, where businesses must adapt quickly to stay competitive.

APIs are a fundamental component of modern software architecture, facilitating communication between applications, enhancing operational efficiency, and driving innovation in the business world. They allow the same code or functions to be used in different parts of the software, while hiding the internal complexity of the system and divide large systems into smaller, easier-to-manage parts, allowing parts of a system to be added or changed without affecting its operation. Their ability to connect disparate systems makes them indispensable for organizations looking to leverage technology to achieve their goals.

Automation: Streamlining Processes

Automation is a transformative process that leverages technology to execute tasks with minimal human involvement. This spectrum of automation can vary significantly, encompassing everything from straightforward, repetitive tasks such as data entry or scheduling to intricate operations that may involve complex algorithms and machine learning.

The primary goal of automation is to enhance efficiency and productivity, allowing individuals and organizations to focus on more strategic activities rather than mundane tasks.

Recognizing Automation Triggers

Every automation process begins with a trigger, which is the event that initiates the automated action. Identifying the correct trigger involves understanding what prompts the task. For example:

- Updating sales database could be triggered every hour, ensuring that the strategical decision-making considers real-time information.

- Sending a thank-you email after a purchase could be triggered by payment confirmation, enhancing customer engagement and satisfaction.

Understanding triggers is essential for creating effective automation workflows that respond to specific events or actions. They are defined and adapted according to the automated solution needed and the system available to implement it.

They could be differentiated into three types:

- **Home Automation Systems:** Technologies like Amazon Alexa and Google Home have revolutionized how we manage our daily routines. These systems can control lighting, temperature, security, and even appliances through voice commands or smartphone apps, making life more convenient and energy efficient. For instance, you can set your thermostat to adjust automatically based on your schedule or have your coffee maker start brewing as soon as your alarm goes off.

- **Workplace Automation:** In professional settings, automation tools are increasingly used to streamline processes. For example, email management systems can automatically sort and prioritize emails based on their content, helping employees focus on the most critical communications. Additionally, project management tools can automate task assignments and reminders, ensuring that teams stay on track without constant oversight.

- **Code/No-code Tools:** These platforms have democratized automation, allowing individuals without extensive programming knowledge to create their own automated workflows. No-code tools enable users to build applications and automate processes through intuitive interfaces, while low-code platforms provide a bit more flexibility for those who may have some coding skills but do not want to write extensive code.

Platforms like Monica and Make or Cody are today (2024) popular choices for creating simple automations. For instance, Monica allows users to connect different applications and automate tasks such as automatically saving email attachments to cloud storage or posting social media updates based on specific triggers.

When choosing between no-code tools and custom coding solutions, several factors should be considered. Cost-effectiveness is a significant advantage of no-code tools, as they often require lower upfront investment and maintenance costs compared to custom-built solutions.

However, organizations must also evaluate the integration capabilities of these tools with their existing systems. While no-code solutions can be quick to implement, they may not always offer the same level of customization and scalability as bespoke coding solutions, which can be tailored to meet specific business needs.

Evaluating Automation Potential

To determine whether a task is suitable for automation, consider the following factors:

- **Duration of Manual Completion**: Assess how long it takes to complete the task manually. Tasks that are time-consuming and repetitive are prime candidates for automation.

- **Timing Requirements**: Identify when the task needs to be completed. If a task has strict deadlines or needs to occur at specific intervals, automation can ensure timely execution.

- **Frequency of Task**: Evaluate how often the task is performed. High-frequency tasks are more likely to benefit from automation, as the time saved can accumulate significantly over time.

- **Automation Setup Time**: Estimate the time required to create the automation. If the setup time is reasonable compared to the time saved, it may be worth pursuing.

- **Operational Costs**: Consider the cost implications of running the automated process. Analyze whether the long-term savings from automation outweigh the initial investment and ongoing operational costs.

- **Ensured data regulations:** Compliance with regulations is crucial. Your business must be able to incorporate a logical step in the automation that can verify customer consent as needed before proceeding, safeguarding against potential legal issues, and building trust with customers. Be aware of local and international terms.

Automation is a powerful tool that can significantly improve efficiency and productivity across various aspects of life and work. With the rise of no-code and low-code platforms, more individuals and organizations can harness the benefits of automation without needing extensive technical expertise.

However, careful consideration of the specific needs and capabilities of these tools is essential for successful implementation. However, if the task involves only a single run, manual completion might be more efficient, highlighting the importance of evaluating the frequency and scale of tasks before diving into any solution.

Chatbots: Revolutionizing Customer Interaction

Chatbots are sophisticated software applications specifically designed to simulate conversation with human users, often through text or voice interactions. They play a crucial role in automating customer interactions across various platforms, such as websites, messaging apps, and social media. By providing quick and efficient responses, chatbots significantly reduce wait times for users, enhancing the overall customer experience.

These systems are designed to handle conversations that do not necessitate human involvement, thereby streamlining operational processes and significantly enhancing overall efficiency. In short, the machine can effectively respond to inquiries that have traditionally been managed by human agents, they are meticulously engineered to tackle real-world challenges by automating routine interactions, which not only saves time but also reduces operational costs.

Basic Functionality

At their core, chatbots operate on an "if-then" logic, which allows them to guide users through a series of predefined options. They function by accurately discerning user intentions based on their inputs and guiding them through a predefined journey tailored to their needs. This means that when a user inputs a specific query or command, the chatbot can respond with a predetermined answer or direct the user to the next step in a process. This basic functionality is particularly useful for handling frequently asked questions, booking appointments, or providing information about products and services.

This automated process not only conserves time for both the user and the business but also optimizes resource allocation by minimizing the reliance on human operators.

It works in three steps:

1. **User Intent Recognition:** To identify what the user is seeking and guide them, accordingly, ensuring a smooth interaction.

2. **Automated Questioning:** Ask necessary follow-up questions to clarify the user's needs when needed.

3. **Task Completion:** After gathering all required information, the chatbot autonomously completes the task, whether it involves providing information, processing requests, or scheduling appointments.

Advanced Capabilities

With advancements in technology, chatbots have progressed far beyond simple multiple-choice interactions. Many now incorporate NLP capabilities allowing them to handle user queries in a more human-like manner, enabling them to respond to a wider range of questions without relying solely on predefined options.

NLP empowers chatbots to engage in more dynamic conversations, making them more effective in addressing complex inquiries and providing personalized responses based on user intent, which greatly enhances user experience by allowing users to communicate in a more intuitive and conversational manner.

This advancement is largely driven by artificial intelligence and machine learning technologies:

- **Natural Language Processing:** This technology enables chatbots to comprehend user inputs expressed in everyday language, making interactions feel more natural and less robotic.

- **Machine Learning:** Chatbots continuously learn from interactions, improving their response accuracy and relevance over time, which leads to a more effective user experience.

- **Enhanced User Experience:** By reducing the need for users to navigate through extensive options, chatbots streamline the interaction process, making it more user-friendly.

Business Impact

The implementation of chatbots can have a significant positive impact on businesses. By efficiently handling customer inquiries, chatbots free up human agents to focus on more complex issues that require personal attention, allowing business owners to redirect their focus towards core activities that drive growth and innovation. This not only enhances customer service but also improves operational efficiency.

Additionally, chatbots can provide valuable insights into customer behavior and preferences, allowing businesses to tailor their services and marketing strategies accordingly.

Considering how important customers are to all business, chatbots can efficiently manage the following inquiries and even escalate more complex issues when necessary, showing how versatile and effective they can be in real-world scenarios:

- **Greeting and Query Handling**: The chatbot initiates interaction with a message, setting tone expected for the conversation (Casual, formal, friendly u other).

- **FAQ Management**: It provides instant answers to common questions, reducing waiting times for customers.

- **Appointment Booking:** Collects necessary details from users and confirms bookings automatically.

- **Escalation Protocols:** In cases where queries are too complex for the chatbot to handle, it can seamlessly transfer the conversation to a human representative, ensuring that customer needs are met.

Overall, the integration of chatbots into customer service frameworks can lead to increased customer satisfaction, loyalty, and ultimately, higher revenue and efficiency.

Businesses stand to benefit from streamlined operations, while customers enjoy swift and reliable responses to their inquiries. As technology continues to advance, chatbots are poised to play an increasingly crucial role in enhancing business communication strategies, making them an invaluable asset for organizations of all sizes.

Practical AI integration Case: Food & Service

The integration of artificial intelligence, automation, and chatbots has the potential to revolutionize operational efficiency across multiple sectors, with the restaurant industry being a prime example.

By leveraging these technologies, restaurants can enhance their service delivery, optimize resource management, and ultimately improve customer satisfaction.

- **Automating Reservation Systems Using Chatbots:** Chatbots can be programmed to handle reservation requests seamlessly. Customers can interact with the chatbot via the restaurant's website or social media platforms to book tables, modify reservations, or receive confirmations. This automation reduces the workload on staff, minimizes human error, and provides customers with instant responses, enhancing their overall experience.

- **Utilizing AI for Inventory Management and Demand Forecasting:** AI algorithms can analyze historical sales data, seasonal trends, and customer preferences to predict future demand accurately. This capability allows restaurants to manage their inventory more effectively, ensuring that they have the right amount of stock on hand while reducing waste. By optimizing inventory levels, restaurants can save costs and improve their profitability.

- **Streamlining Order Processing with Integrated APIs:** Can facilitate smoother communication between various systems used in a restaurant, such as point-of-sale (POS) systems, kitchen display systems, and delivery platforms allowing for real-time updates on orders, reducing waiting times, and improving order accuracy.

As technology rapidly evolves, its integration into business processes is essential for organizations to stay competitive. The adoption of advanced technologies like artificial intelligence, automation, APIs, and chatbots is crucial for enhancing efficiency and fostering innovation. AI can transform decision-making by analyzing data to predict customer behavior and optimize operations, leading to improved satisfaction and revenue.

In summary, Automation streamlines repetitive tasks, reducing errors and costs while allowing employees to focus on strategic initiatives. APIs enable seamless communication between software applications, enhancing adaptability and service offerings. Chatbots revolutionize customer service by providing instant support, improving customer experience, and optimizing resource allocation.

The practical application of these technologies best practices to help businesses harness their potential for growth and innovation in a digital landscape.

Chapter 2

Integrating AI into Your Business: A Strategic Guide

Artificial Intelligence is revolutionizing industries, transforming how businesses operate, and creating opportunities for increased efficiency, better decision-making, and enhanced customer experiences.

However, successfully integrating AI into your business requires more than just adopting the technology, as we have seen before, it demands careful planning, strategic alignment with business goals, and a commitment to continuous improvement.

AI has the potential to significantly enhance business performance across various sectors, but its success hinges on thoughtful and strategic implementation. Organizations must recognize that poorly planned AI initiatives can lead to a multitude of challenges, including wasted resources, missed opportunities for innovation, and even reputational risks that can tarnish a brand's image.

For instance, if an AI system is not aligned with the company's goals or is implemented without proper training and support, it may fail to deliver the expected results, leading to frustration among employees and stakeholders, as well as triggering distrust about the culture of innovation.

On the contrary, a well-executed AI strategy can unlock transformative benefits that drive a business forward. This includes improved operational efficiency, enhanced decision-making abilities, and the ability to offer personalized customer experience. By leveraging AI technologies such as machine learning, natural language processing, and data analytics, companies can gain valuable insights into market trends, customer behavior, and internal processes. This data-driven approach enables organizations to make informed decisions, optimize their resources, and ultimately drive growth.

Moreover, successful AI implementation requires a collaborative effort across various departments, including IT, operations, and management. It is essential to foster a culture of innovation and continuous learning, where employees are encouraged to embrace new technologies and adapt to changing market dynamics.

By investing in training and development, businesses can ensure that their workforce is equipped with the necessary skills to harness the power of AI effectively.

So, effective AI implementation is not just about adopting technology, but it is about aligning it with your business objectives to create meaningful impact. By planning carefully and addressing potential challenges upfront, you can unlock AI's full potential.

While it holds immense potential to revolutionize your performance, its success is contingent upon careful planning, alignment with organizational goals, and a commitment to fostering a culture of innovation. By taking these factors into account, companies can position themselves to reap the rewards of AI and stay competitive in an increasingly digital landscape.

Key Benefits of Effective AI Implementation

- **Maximizing ROI:** Proper integration ensures your investment delivers measurable returns. For instance, any AI-powered recommendation engine has increased user engagement and retention, driving higher subscription rates.

- **Minimizing Risks:** Thoughtful planning helps address challenges like data privacy, algorithmic bias, and integration issues. Retail banks, for example, use AI for fraud detection while maintaining robust governance frameworks to reduce false positives.

- **Gaining a Competitive Edge:** Leveraging AI for operational efficiency and customer satisfaction can set your business apart. Amazon's AI-driven supply chain optimization has enhanced delivery speeds and reduced costs.

- **Improving Customer Service:** AI-powered tools like chatbots handle routine queries efficiently, freeing up human agents for complex issues. Banks use these tools to provide real-time customer support, improving satisfaction levels.

Steps to Implement AI Successfully

Implementing AI involves more than just deploying a tool; it is about integrating it seamlessly into your business processes. This integration requires a comprehensive understanding of both the technology and the specific needs of your organization.

Here is a step-by-step guide to ensure success in your AI implementation journey:

1. **Define Clear Objectives:** This could range from improving customer service through chatbots to optimizing supply chain management. Clear objectives will guide your implementation strategy.
    - Identify specific and detail problems AI can solve and set the expectation for it.
    - Align these goals with broader business objectives.

2. **Business "hard-ware":** Evaluate your existing technology stack and data infrastructure. Look if your current systems allows AI integration or if it needs upgrades.

- Review where and how AI can really add value.
- Focus on repetitive or error-prone tasks that AI can automate and demand less human intervention.

3. **Business "soft-ware":** Ensure necessary skills to work with AI technologies and encourage a culture that embraces technology and innovation within your organization. This may involve training sessions, workshops, or hiring new talent with expertise in AI and data science. A knowledgeable team with innovation mindset is crucial for successful implementation of any emerging technology and ongoing management.
   - Measures your team's ability to adapt and learn, both individually and as a group.
   - Estimate the expected impact of the implementation on the company, in terms of results and time. It should be proportional to the team and resources available.

4. **You are your data:** AI systems rely heavily on data. Gather relevant data from various sources within your organization. Ensure that the data is clean, well-organized, and representative of the scenarios you want the AI to address. This may involve data cleansing, normalization, segmentation, and labeling.
   - Identify internal and external data sources (e.g., sales, costs, CRM systems, market research, supplies).
   - Standardize data formats for consistency to ensure data quality through regular cleaning and validation.
   - Centralize data storage using platforms like Google Cloud or AWS.
   - Implement strong data governance policies to manage access and compliance.

5. **Look in to how:** Research and select AI tools and platforms that align with your objectives and infrastructure. Consider factors such as scalability, ease of use, and compatibility with your existing systems.

Popular options include machine learning frameworks, natural language processing tools, and computer vision software.
- Always check the available platforms first. New technologies are always evolving, and there may be one that covers your needs and technical expertise.
- Align the right tools with the right team according to the business objectives.

6. **To be great, start small:** Before a full-scale rollout, create a pilot program to test the AI solution in a controlled environment. This allows you to identify potential issues, gather feedback, and make necessary adjustments without disrupting your entire operation.
   - Define clear measurable quantitative and qualitative KPIs (e.g., reducing overstocking by 20% in one warehouse or good customer reviews).
   - Monitor performance metrics, gather feedback for refinement and check for bias.
   - Create new KPIs or change them within the trial as they reflect results that honestly show the AI performance and ways to improve.

7. **It is time:** Once you achieve success with the pilot, consider scaling the implementation across other areas of your business. Based on the insights gained from monitoring, iterate constantly on your AI solution to enhance its capabilities and continuously monitor the AI system's performance against your defined objectives. Use key performance indicators to evaluate its effectiveness and make data-driven decisions for improvements, as we will see in detail next.
   - Choose the trainers wisely to expand the pilot projects across your organization.
   - Look for a training pyramid to streamline the process of implementation. Each team will be impacted according to their needs.
   - Never stop monitoring performance and adjusting.

By following these steps, you can ensure that your AI initiatives are strategic, impactful, and aligned with your business goals. Start small, learn from pilot projects, and scale up thoughtfully for long-term success.

Measuring the Impact of AI on Your Business

Once you have implemented AI within your organization, measuring its impact becomes a crucial step in understanding not only its effectiveness but also in optimizing its ongoing use. This process involves a comprehensive evaluation of various metrics and key performance indicators (KPIs) that can provide insights into how well the AI system is performing in relation to your business objectives.

By systematically analyzing the data generated by the AI, you can determine whether it is delivering the expected outcomes and tangible value. This could include improvements in efficiency, cost savings, enhanced customer satisfaction, or increased revenue.

Furthermore, understanding the impact of AI allows you to identify areas where the technology may be falling short, enabling you to make informed adjustments or enhancements.

Additionally, measuring the impact of AI is not just a one-time task; it should be an ongoing process that informs future decisions. By continuously monitoring performance and gathering feedback, you can refine your AI strategies, ensuring that they align with evolving business goals and market conditions.

With the following insights this iterative approach not only maximizes the return on your investment but also positions your organization to leverage AI more effectively in the long run.

Track Key Metrics

- **Productivity:** Measure task completion rates or work volume increases.

- **Cost Efficiency:** Track savings from reduced labor costs or error rates.

- **Revenue Growth:** Analyze sales increases from AI-driven recommendations.

- **Process Optimization:** Identify bottlenecks resolved by AI.

- **Customer Satisfaction:** Use metrics like Net Promoter Scores (NPS) or customer feedback ratings.

Use Live Data Visualization Tools

Platforms like Tableau or Power BI can display real-time performance metrics, enabling quick decision-making. These platforms can connect to various data sources, such as databases, spreadsheets, and cloud services, to aggregate and display performance metrics dynamically. Users can create interactive dashboards that provide insights into key performance indicators (KPIs), trends, and patterns within the data. They can also create reports and dashboards that are easily shareable across the organization, ensuring that stakeholders have access to the latest data.

These platforms support real-time data updates, meaning that as new data comes in, the visualizations automatically refresh to reflect the most current information, ready to use and operate in fast-paced environments where quick decision-making is essential.

Foster Continuous Improvement

Measuring the impact of AI is an ongoing process that ensures your initiatives continue to deliver value. By using data-driven insights, you can optimize performance and build confidence, and by using qualitative data you can perceive culture, communication, and relationships between all the stakeholders.
- Collect feedback from all stakeholders, employees, and customers.
- Conduct regular audits of AI systems to ensure they remain effective.
- Stay updated on advancements in AI technology to refine your strategy.

Leveraging AI for Process Optimization

AI is a powerful tool for streamlining workflows, reducing inefficiencies, and driving continuous improvement across various industries. By leveraging advanced algorithms and machine learning techniques, businesses can automate repetitive tasks, analyze vast amounts of data, and make informed decisions in real-time. This not only enhances productivity but also allows employees to focus on more strategic initiatives that require human creativity and critical thinking.

Moreover, businesses that embrace process optimization through AI gain a significant competitive advantage. They can operate more efficiently by minimizing errors, speeding up processes, and improving overall service delivery. For instance, AI can help in predictive maintenance, where it anticipates equipment failures before they occur, thus reducing downtime and maintenance costs.

Additionally, AI-driven analytics can provide insights into customer behavior, enabling companies to tailor their offerings and improve customer satisfaction. By understanding market trends and consumer preferences businesses can innovate and adapt more quickly than their competitors.

The integration of AI into business processes not only streamlines operations but also fosters a culture of continuous improvement, ultimately leading to enhanced performance and growth in a competitive landscape. Here are the main practical applications:

- **Identify Inefficiencies:** Use AI to analyze large datasets and uncover hidden patterns or bottlenecks.

- **Automate Repetitive Tasks:** Free up employees for strategic work by automating manual processes.

- **Monitor and Refine Processes:** Continuously analyze real-time data to adjust workflows and improve efficiency.

- **Foster a Culture of Innovation:** Involve employees in identifying areas for improvement and implementing solutions. Transparency and collaboration lead to better outcomes.

Process optimization through AI is not a one-time effort but an ongoing journey. By continuously refining workflows and engaging employees in the process, businesses can achieve sustained efficiency gains and long-term success.

As we have seen, in summary the integration of AI into your business is a transformative opportunity that requires strategic planning, thoughtful execution, and continuous refinement. By defining clear objectives, leveraging the right tools and talent, measuring impact, and fostering a culture of innovation, you can harness the full potential of AI to drive growth, efficiency, and customer satisfaction.

Take the first step today, evaluate your goals, identify key challenges, and start exploring how AI can revolutionize your business processes. The future of your business starts now!

Chapter 3

Unlocking AI's Business Potential

Artificial Intelligence has emerged as a transformative force across various industries, fundamentally altering the way businesses operate and deliver value. By harnessing advanced algorithms and machine learning techniques, AI has the capability to analyze vast amounts of data at unprecedented speeds, enabling organizations to make informed decisions based on real-time insights.

One of the most significant advantages of AI is its ability to streamline and automate processes that were once time-consuming and labor-intensive.

For instance, in manufacturing, AI-driven robots can perform repetitive tasks with precision, reducing the likelihood of human error and increasing overall productivity. In the realm of customer service, AI chatbots can handle inquiries and provide support 24/7, enhancing customer satisfaction while freeing up human agents to tackle more complex issues.

Moreover, AI's predictive analytics capabilities allow businesses to anticipate market trends and consumer behavior, leading to more effective marketing strategies and product development. By analyzing historical data, AI can identify patterns and forecast future outcomes, enabling companies to stay ahead of the competition.

In addition to operational efficiency, AI fosters innovation by enabling the development of new products and services. For example, in the healthcare sector, AI algorithms can assist in diagnosing diseases and personalizing treatment plans, ultimately improving patient outcomes. Similarly, in finance, AI can detect fraudulent activities and assess credit risks more accurately than traditional methods.

As AI continues to evolve, its applications are becoming increasingly diverse, making it an indispensable tool for modern businesses seeking to thrive in a rapidly changing landscape. The integration of AI not only enhances operational capabilities but also drives strategic growth, positioning organizations for long-term success in an increasingly competitive market.

The purpose of this guide is to help you explore how AI can transform your business operations and help you achieve your goals more effectively, and we will concentrate on the three main aspects where AI can provide substantial benefits: improving efficiency, predicting trends, and customizing experiences.

Boosting Efficiency with Automation

Imagine a scenario where your team is liberated from the burden of repetitive and mundane tasks, allowing them to channel their energy and creativity into more strategic and innovative projects. This transformation is not just a dream; it is a tangible reality made possible by the advancements in artificial intelligence.

AI technology provides a robust solution that can significantly streamline various processes within your organization. By automating routine tasks, AI minimizes the likelihood of human errors, which can often lead to costly mistakes and inefficiencies. This reduction in errors not only enhances the quality of work but also nurtures a more reliable workflow.

Moreover, the implementation of AI tools can lead to a substantial boost in overall productivity. With less time spent on repetitive tasks, team members can dedicate their efforts to high-impact projects that require critical thinking and creativity. This shift not only improves job satisfaction among employees but also drives innovation within the organization, as teams are empowered to explore new ideas and solutions.

Practical Steps to Implement Automation:

1. **Identify Repetitive Tasks:** Begin by conducting a thorough evaluation of your current operations to pinpoint specific tasks that are repetitive and time-consuming but do not require deep human expertise. These tasks often include activities such as data entry, sorting information, and other administrative duties that can drain valuable resources. By identifying these tasks, you can create a clear picture of where automation can be most beneficial.

2. **Leverage AI Tools for Automation:** Once you have identified the repetitive tasks, the next step is to leverage AI-powered software to automate these processes. For example, logistics companies like SpeedSort have successfully implemented AI technology to automate package sorting. This not only significantly reduces the time required for sorting packages but also enhances accuracy in the sorting process. As a result, employees are freed up to focus on more critical areas such as customer service and strategic planning, which are essential for business growth and customer satisfaction.

3. **Monitor and Optimize:** After implementing AI tools, it is crucial to continuously monitor their performance to ensure they are delivering the desired results. This involves tracking key performance indicators (KPIs) and gathering feedback from employees who interact with the AI systems. By regularly assessing the effectiveness of these tools, you can make informed adjustments to workflows and processes as needed. This ongoing optimization helps to maximize efficiency and ensures that the automation remains aligned with your business goals.

By automating routine activities using AI tools, you can significantly enhance your operational efficiency. This allows your team to allocate their energy and resources toward high-value tasks that drive innovation and growth within your organization. Embracing automation not only streamlines processes but also empowers your workforce to focus on strategic initiatives that can lead to long-term success.

Predicting Trends with Data Insights

What if you could foresee market trends or customer behavior before they happen? The integration of Artificial Intelligence into business operations has revolutionized the way companies approach decision-making. AI empowers businesses with predictive analytics, a powerful tool that enables smarter decision-making based on data-driven forecasts.

By leveraging vast amounts of data, organizations can gain insights that were previously unattainable, allowing them to stay ahead of the competition and respond proactively to market changes.

Practical Steps to Predictive Analytics

1. **Gather Historical Data:** The first step in utilizing predictive analytics is to collect historical data from various sources. This includes sales records, customer interactions, market reports, and any other relevant data points. The quality and comprehensiveness of this data are crucial, as it forms the foundation for AI's analysis. Businesses should ensure that they are capturing data consistently and accurately to maximize the effectiveness of their predictive models.

2. **Train AI Models:** Once the data is gathered, the next step is to train AI models using machine learning algorithms. These algorithms analyze the data to identify patterns and correlations that might not be obvious to human analysts. By employing techniques such as regression analysis, decision trees, and neural networks, businesses can develop models that predict future outcomes based on historical trends. This process often involves iterative testing and refinement to improve the accuracy of the predictions.

3. **Make Informed Decisions:** With trained AI models, businesses can apply insights from predictive analytics to optimize their operations. For example, airlines like SkyFly utilize AI to predict maintenance needs and prevent delays by analyzing historical flight data and weather patterns. By anticipating potential issues before they arise, SkyFly has successfully reduced disruptions by up to 80%, significantly improving customer satisfaction and operational efficiency. This proactive approach allows companies to allocate resources more effectively and enhance overall performance.

4. **Anticipate Customer Needs:** Retailers such as ShopSmart leverage predictive analytics to forecast demand for products, ensuring that inventory levels are adjusted proactively. By analyzing purchasing patterns, seasonal trends, and external factors, ShopSmart can minimize stockouts and overstocking, leading to better inventory management and increased sales. This capability not only enhances customer experience by ensuring product availability but also optimizes supply chain operations.

In today's fast-paced business environment, predictive analytics equips your organization with the foresight needed to stay ahead of competitors, mitigate risks, and seize opportunities. By harnessing the power of AI and predictive analytics, businesses can transform their decision-making processes, leading to improved outcomes and sustained growth. Embracing these technologies is no longer a luxury but a necessity for companies aiming to thrive in an increasingly data-driven world.

Personalizing Customer Experiences

In today's competitive market, personalization is key to winning customer loyalty. With the rapid advancement of technology, particularly artificial intelligence, businesses could tailor their offerings to meet individual preferences and needs. This level of customization not only creates memorable and engaging experiences for customers but also fosters a deeper connection between the brand and its audience.

As consumers increasingly expect personalized interactions, companies that leverage AI to enhance their customer experience are more likely to stand out in a crowded marketplace.

Practical Steps for Personalization:

1. **Analyze Customer Behavior:** To effectively personalize offerings, businesses must first understand their customers. Utilizing AI tools to study customer interactions, purchase history, and preferences is essential. For instance, streaming platforms like Spotify employ sophisticated algorithms to analyze listening habits, enabling them to recommend personalized playlists that resonate with individual users. This data-driven approach allows companies to gain insights into customer behavior, leading to more informed decision-making and targeted marketing strategies.

2. **Deliver Tailored Recommendations:** Once businesses have a clear understanding of their customers, they can implement recommendation systems that suggest products or services based on the analyzed data. For example, online retailers often use AI to analyze browsing patterns and past purchases, allowing them to suggest items that customers are likely to buy. This not only boosts sales but also enhances customer engagement by providing a seamless shopping experience. By offering personalized

recommendations, businesses can increase conversion rates and foster customer loyalty.

3. **Enhance Employee Feedback Systems:** Personalization is not limited to customer interactions; it can also be applied internally within organizations. AI can be utilized to personalize feedback for employees by analyzing performance metrics and individual contributions. This tailored approach helps employees understand their strengths and areas for improvement, ultimately aiding them in achieving their professional goals. By fostering a culture of personalized feedback, companies can enhance employee satisfaction and productivity, leading to a more motivated workforce.

Personalization powered by AI is a transformative strategy that not only strengthens customer relationships but also enhances employee satisfaction and productivity. By analyzing customer behavior, delivering tailored recommendations, and personalizing internal feedback systems, businesses can create a more engaging and fulfilling experience for both external and internal clients of the company. As the market continues to evolve, those who embrace AI-driven personalization will be well-positioned to thrive in an increasingly competitive landscape.

AI's potential is vast, but its true power lies in how you use it strategically within your business. Start by identifying specific goals or challenges where AI can make a difference, whether it is improving efficiency, anticipating market changes, or delivering personalized experiences. By embracing AI thoughtfully, you will position your business for long-term success in an increasingly competitive landscape.

Chapter 4

Crafting Your AI Game Plan

In the constantly changing landscape of business, keeping a competitive edge and the adoption of innovative technologies is a must, staying ahead of the curve requires embracing transformative technologies.

Not too long ago, Apple introduced the iPhone, which transformed the way people interacted with technology. Before smartphones, mobile devices were limited in functionality, often requiring users to navigate clunky menus or memorize complex commands. The iPhone's intuitive touchscreen interface and app ecosystem made mobile technology accessible to everyone, revolutionizing industries, and daily life.

The impact of AI today parallels the transformative potential of the smartphone era. Just as businesses adapted to the opportunities created by mobile technology, they now have the chance to embrace AI as a powerful tool to enhance productivity and efficiency.

AI holds the promise to reshape operations, improve customer experiences, and solve intricate challenges. From automating routine tasks to providing predictive insights, AI can help businesses achieve their goals more effectively. However, integrating AI thoughtfully into your strategy is key to maximizing its benefits.

By thoughtfully integrating AI into your business strategy, you can unlock its full potential to solve challenges, streamline operations, and drive growth.

In the following, you will find the comprehensive steps to create a successful AI roadmap that is specifically tailored to meet the unique needs and objectives of your business. This roadmap will guide you through the process of integrating artificial intelligence into your operations, ensuring that you leverage the technology effectively to enhance productivity, improve decision-making, and drive innovation.

Why AI is the Next Big Step for Your Business

AI is not just a buzzword, it is a powerful tool that can reshape industries. Think of it as the next wave of innovation, similar to how earlier technologies simplified complex systems and opened new opportunities. By adopting AI, businesses can automate repetitive tasks, make smarter decisions using data-driven insights, and deliver more personalized experiences to customers.

What can AI do for your business?

- Automate routine processes to save time and reduce costs.
- Enhance decision-making with predictive analytics.
- Improve customer experiences through personalization.
- Stay competitive with faster, data-informed strategies.

Setting Clear Objectives: Defining Your AI Vision

A clear vision is the foundation of any successful AI strategy. It serves as a guiding light that directs all efforts and resources towards achieving specific objectives. Before diving into the complexities of AI implementation, it is crucial to take a step back and identify what you want to achieve. This involves a thorough analysis of your current business landscape, understanding the challenges you face, and recognizing the opportunities that AI can unlock.

Consider the various aspects of your organization where AI could make a significant impact. This could range from enhancing customer experience through personalized recommendations to optimizing operational efficiencies by automating routine tasks. By clearly defining your goals, you can better assess how AI technologies can be leveraged to meet those objectives.

Moreover, this initial step ensures that your AI initiatives align with your broader business goals. It is essential to ensure that the AI strategy is not developed in isolation but rather integrates seamlessly with the overall vision and mission of the organization. This alignment helps in securing buy-in from stakeholders and ensures that resources are allocated effectively.

In summary, taking the time to establish a clear vision for your AI strategy is not just a preliminary step; it is a critical component that lays the groundwork for successful implementation and long-term sustainability of AI initiatives within your organization.

How to define your AI goals:

- **Be specific.** Instead of setting a vague objective like "improve customer service," it is crucial to aim for measurable outcomes that can be tracked and evaluated over time. For instance, you could set a goal to reduce response times by 40%, which would involve analyzing current response metrics and implementing strategies to enhance efficiency.

- **Focus on areas with high impact.** Identifying and prioritizing initiatives that can significantly influence overall performance is essential. This could involve streamlining operations by assessing current workflows and eliminating bottlenecks, which can lead to faster service delivery and reduced costs.

Example: A leading online retailer used AI to optimize its delivery systems and warehouse operations. By implementing machine learning algorithms, they reduce delivery times and costs while improving customer satisfaction. Their use of predictive analytics also minimize waste by accurately forecasting customer demand.

Building a Strong Data Foundation

AI thrives on high-quality data, which serves as the foundation for its learning and decision-making processes. To maximize its potential, businesses must establish a robust data management strategy that encompasses several key components. This strategy should ensure accuracy, meaning that the data collected and utilized is correct and free from errors.

Consistency is also crucial; data should be uniform across different systems and platforms to avoid discrepancies that could lead to flawed insights. Additionally, security is paramount, as businesses must protect sensitive information from breaches and unauthorized access.

By focusing on these elements, organizations can create a data environment that not only supports AI initiatives but also drives overall business success. Implementing best practices in data governance, regular audits, and employee training on data handling can further enhance the effectiveness of the data management strategy.

Steps to create a data strategy:

1. **Identify all sources of business data:** This involves conducting a comprehensive audit of all data-generating activities within the organization. Sources may include sales transactions, customer

interactions through various channels (such as email, social media, and customer service), supply chain logistics, inventory management systems, and any other relevant operational data. Understanding where data originates is crucial for building a robust data strategy.

2. **Ensure data is clean, consistent, and relevant to your AI goals:** Data quality is paramount for effective AI implementation. This step includes data cleansing processes to remove duplicates, correct inaccuracies, and fill in missing values. Consistency across datasets is also essential, meaning that data formats, units of measurement, and naming conventions should be standardized. Additionally, the data must be relevant to the specific objectives of the AI initiatives, ensuring that it can effectively inform decision-making and model training.

3. **Implement secure storage and management systems:** Data security is critical, especially when handling sensitive information. Organizations should invest in secure storage solutions, such as encrypted databases and cloud services with robust security protocols. Data management systems should also be established to facilitate easy access, retrieval, and analysis of data while maintaining security and compliance with regulations.

4. **Establish governance policies to ensure compliance and protect sensitive information:** Governance policies are necessary to outline how data is managed, accessed, and shared within the organization. This includes defining roles and responsibilities for data stewardship, implementing access controls, and ensuring compliance with relevant regulations (such as GDPR or HIPAA). Policies should also address data retention, usage, and disposal to protect sensitive information and mitigate risks associated with data breaches.

Example: A supermarket chain leverages its loyalty program data to enhance the shopping experience for its customers. By examining the buying patterns and preferences of loyalty program participants, the supermarket can customize promotions that appeal to individual shoppers. For example, if a customer regularly purchases organic products, the supermarket may offer them targeted discounts on organic items, promoting repeat purchases and building brand loyalty.

Additionally, the supermarket utilizes this data to improve its inventory management. By recognizing which products are favored by various customer segments, the supermarket can ensure it has the right items in appropriate quantities.

This approach not only minimizes waste and prevents stock shortages but also boosts customer satisfaction, as shoppers are more likely to find their desired products available during their visits. Moreover, by spotting trends and preferences, the supermarket can create store layouts, organize marketing campaigns, and introduce new product offerings that cater to customer needs.

This holistic strategy for utilizing data not only aids the supermarket in making well-informed decisions but also improves operational efficiency, resulting in higher sales and customer loyalty.

Leveraging Cost-Effective AI Solutions

A common misconception is that adopting AI is prohibitively expensive or overly complex. However, the landscape of AI tools has evolved significantly in recent years. Today, there is a wide array of user-friendly AI solutions available that are designed to cater to the needs of businesses of all sizes, from small startups to large enterprises.

These tools often come with intuitive interfaces that require minimal technical expertise, allowing users to implement AI solutions without the need for extensive training or specialized knowledge. Many platforms offer scalable options, meaning that businesses can start with basic functionalities and gradually expand their use of AI as they become more comfortable and as their needs grow.

Furthermore, the cost of implementing AI has decreased considerably, with many providers offering flexible pricing models, including subscription-based services and pay-as-you-go options. This accessibility enables businesses to experiment with AI technologies without committing to large upfront investments.

How to adopt AI affordably:

- **Explore third-party platforms:** Many platforms offer AI capabilities that can be integrated seamlessly with existing systems. For instance, customer relationship management (CRM) tools often come with built-in AI features that can enhance customer interactions and streamline processes. By leveraging these platforms, businesses can avoid the high costs associated with developing custom AI solutions from scratch.

- **Start small:** It is advisable for businesses to begin their AI journey with tools that are tailored to specific needs. For example, implementing chatbots for customer service can significantly improve response times and customer satisfaction without requiring a large investment. Similarly, analytics software that utilizes AI for trend predictions can help businesses make data-driven decisions, allowing them to grow gradually as they become more comfortable with the technology.

- **Consider advanced solutions:** As businesses become more familiar with AI, they may want to explore more advanced solutions. In such cases, hiring specialists or partnering with technology providers can be a cost-effective way to access expertise and resources. These professionals can help tailor AI solutions to meet specific business needs, ensuring that the investment yields a strong return.

By taking these insights, businesses can adopt AI in a way that is both affordable and effective, enhancing their operations and competitiveness in the market.

Empowering Your Team with AI Knowledge

Your team's ability to adapt and embrace AI is crucial for long-term success in today's rapidly evolving technological landscape. As businesses increasingly rely on artificial intelligence to enhance efficiency, improve decision-making, and drive innovation, it becomes imperative for your workforce to be well-equipped with the necessary skills and knowledge.

Providing comprehensive training and fostering a culture of innovation not only empowers employees but also ensures that they can identify and seize opportunities to leverage AI effectively within their roles.

Ways to build AI expertise:

- **Offer online courses or workshops on relevant AI tools and technologies:** Investing in online learning platforms that provide courses on machine learning, data analysis, natural language processing, and other AI-related subjects can significantly enhance your team's capabilities. Workshops led by industry experts can also provide hands-on experience and practical insights.

- **Partner with local universities or tech organizations for training programs:** Collaborating with educational institutions or technology organizations can facilitate access to specialized training programs. These partnerships can lead to tailored workshops, guest lectures, and even internship opportunities that allow your team to learn from experienced professionals in the field.

- **Encourage experimentation and continuous learning within your team:** Creating an environment that promotes experimentation with AI technologies can lead to innovative solutions and improvements in processes. Encourage team members to explore new tools, participate in hackathons, and share their findings with the group. Establishing a culture of continuous learning, where employees are motivated to stay updated on the latest AI trends and advancements will further enhance your team's expertise.

By implementing these strategies, you can cultivate a workforce that is not only knowledgeable about AI but also enthusiastic about integrating it into their daily operations, ultimately driving your organization's success in the long run.

Seamlessly Integrating AI into Business Processes

To maximize impact, it is crucial that artificial intelligence is seamlessly integrated into your existing workflows instead of being treated as a separate or standalone initiative.

This approach not only ensures that AI enhances overall efficiency but also aligns with your strategic objectives, creating a more cohesive operational environment.

Organizations can successfully integrate AI into their workflows, leading to improved efficiency, enhanced decision-making, and ultimately, a stronger competitive advantage in the marketplace.

Tips for smooth integration:

- **Begin with pilot projects:** Start by identifying specific areas within your organization where AI can deliver quick wins. These pilot projects should be manageable in scope and designed to demonstrate the value of AI in a tangible way. By focusing on areas with high potential for immediate impact, you can build momentum and gain buy-in from stakeholders.

- **Regularly assess performance:** It is essential to continuously monitor and evaluate the performance of AI initiatives. Establish key performance indicators (KPIs) to measure success and gather data on outcomes. Use this information to refine your approach, adjust as necessary to optimize results and ensure that the AI solutions are meeting their intended goals.

- **Encourage collaboration across departments:** Foster a culture of collaboration among different departments within your organization. This can be achieved by creating cross-functional teams that include members from various areas of expertise. By working together, these teams can ensure that AI initiatives are aligned with the broader organizational strategy and that insights and feedback are shared effectively.

When AI is incorporated into established workflows, it can automate repetitive tasks, provide data-driven insights, and facilitate decision-making processes. This not only saves time but also allows employees to focus on higher-value activities that require human creativity and critical thinking.

In addition, embedding AI into workflows fosters a culture of innovation and adaptability within the organization. Employees become more accustomed to leveraging AI tools, which can lead to increased acceptance and enthusiasm for technology-driven changes. This cultural shift is essential for maximizing the benefits of AI and ensuring that it is viewed as an asset rather than a disruptive force.

The journey toward integrating AI may seem daunting at first, but starting small and staying adaptable will set you on the right path. With thoughtful planning and a focus on aligning AI initiatives with your business goals, even small businesses can harness the power of this transformative technology. Remember, every big leap starts with a single step, embrace the possibilities that AI offers and position your business for a future of innovation and growth.

Chapter 5

Diving in Content Creation with AI

In today's digital age, storytelling remains a powerful tool for engaging audiences. Whether through novels, films, or advertisements, the most impactful stories connect emotionally, leaving a lasting impression. However, crafting such compelling narratives can be challenging, particularly under tight deadlines. This is where Artificial Intelligence emerges as a transformative ally.

AI has evolved beyond being a mere buzzword; it is now a game-changing technology that empowers content creators. By processing vast amounts of data in seconds, AI identifies trends, predicts consumer behavior, and suggests creative approaches that might elude human intuition. Importantly, AI does not aim to replace human creativity but to enhance it, enabling professionals to focus on innovation and storytelling while automating repetitive tasks.

The key advantages of AI in content creation:

- **Data Analysis**: AI has the capability to quickly process and analyze large datasets, which allows content creators to uncover actionable insights. This means that creators can make informed decisions based on trends, audience preferences, and performance metrics, ultimately leading to more effective content strategies.

- **Creative Support**: AI can assist in the creative process by suggesting innovative ideas and approaches to storytelling. This support can help writers and creators overcome writer's block, explore new angles, and enhance the overall creativity of their work.

- **Efficiency**: One of the significant advantages of AI is its ability to automate routine tasks. This includes grammar checks, content formatting, and other repetitive processes that can consume a lot of time. By automating these tasks, creators can focus more on the creative aspects of their work.

- **Enhanced Personalization**: AI enables the tailoring of content to individual preferences and behaviors. By analyzing user data, AI can help creators develop personalized content that resonates with specific audiences, leading to higher engagement and satisfaction.

Overall, AI opens new possibilities for creators, amplifying their ability to connect with audiences on a deeper level. It allows them to navigate the dynamic digital landscape with confidence, leveraging technology to enhance their creative output and effectiveness.

For example, OpenAI's GPT-4 demonstrates how AI can craft coherent and engaging articles on complex topics. Similarly, AI now powers tools that create personalized content experiences and integrate seamlessly into content management systems.

AI significantly boosts human creativity by serving as a virtual assistant that can analyze large volumes of data and produce insights quickly. This efficiency enables creators to dedicate more time and effort to innovative processes instead of getting bogged down by repetitive or tedious tasks. By handling the heavy data lifting, AI allows individuals to explore new ideas and push the boundaries of their creative endeavors.

AI supports creativity mainly in three ways:

- **Streamlined Workflows**: This feature focuses on automating repetitive tasks, which can significantly enhance productivity. For instance, it can handle data analysis, allowing users to quickly process and interpret large datasets without manual intervention. Additionally, it can assist in generating initial content drafts, saving time and effort for content creators who can then refine and personalize the output.

- **Tailored Strategies**: This aspect emphasizes the importance of customizing content strategies based on platform-specific requirements. It analyzes various content formats and determines which ones are most effective for different social media platforms, websites, or marketing channels. By doing so, it helps marketers and content creators optimize their approach, ensuring that their messages are delivered in the most engaging and impactful way possible.

- **Informed Decision-Making**: This feature provides valuable insights into audience preferences and behaviors. By analyzing data on what types of content resonate with specific demographics, it enables businesses to make data-driven decisions. This can lead to more effective marketing campaigns, improved audience engagement, and ultimately, better conversion rates as strategies are aligned with audience interests.

For instance, an AI tool can analyze platform-specific performance metrics to determine whether videos or infographics perform better on a particular social media channel. This allows creators to allocate resources more effectively and craft content that drives greater engagement.

The practical applications of AI-powered tools are unnumbered. AI-powered platforms are revolutionizing content creation across various mediums. For example, some tools simplify graphic design by offering AI-driven suggestions for layouts, color schemes, and resizing designs for different platforms. Similarly, voice synthesis tools generate realistic voiceovers, reducing the need for expensive recording sessions. Others can help generate articles, headlines, and more. Yet they will never replace the human creativity that occurs through the context, intention, direction, and emotion that is given to the content.

Transforming Content Strategies with AI Solutions

The integration of Artificial Intelligence into content creation has transformed how businesses and creators develop, optimize, and distribute their content. With a wide array of tools available, AI enables users to streamline workflows, enhance creativity, and achieve their goals more efficiently.

Here are the essential stages of content creation ensuring a smooth and productive process. This guide will break down the key stages of content creation, which typically include brainstorming, drafting, editing, and distribution. At each of these stages, various AI-powered tools can help. By leveraging these AI tools throughout the content creation process, users can ensure a more streamlined and productive experience, ultimately leading to higher quality content and better results.

1. **Identifying Your Niche and Target Audience:** Understanding your audience is the foundation of impactful content creation. This involves pinpointing a specific market segment, analyzing audience demographics, and uncovering their interests and challenges.

2. **Defining the Problem or Need:** Effective content addresses the specific problems or needs of the audience. By identifying these pain points, creators can tailor their messages to resonate deeply.

3. **Conducting Research:** Thorough research lays the groundwork for creating content that stands out. This step involves analyzing trends, competitor strategies, and audience interests.

4. **Developing a Content Strategy:** A well-structured content strategy ensures consistency and goal alignment. This includes creating a content calendar, setting objectives, and planning publication timelines.

5. **Brainstorming and Conceptualizing Ideas:** Generating creative ideas and organizing them effectively is crucial for impactful content creation.

6. **Designing Visuals:** Engaging visuals are integral to capturing attention and reinforcing brand identity. They should align with the brand's aesthetic and message.

7. **Writing Engaging Content:** Clear, concise, and engaging writing forms the backbone of any content strategy. Incorporating SEO best practices from the outset ensures visibility.

8. **Optimizing Search Engines (SEO):** SEO ensures that content reaches its intended audience by improving visibility on search engines.

9. **Scheduling Social Media Posts:** Strategic distribution of content across social platforms maximizes reach and engagement.

10. **Engaging with Your Community:** Building a loyal audience requires active engagement through comments, messages, polls, and live sessions.

11. **Analyzing Performance Metrics:** Tracking performance metrics provides valuable insights into audience preferences and content effectiveness.

12. **Repurposing Content for Maximum Reach:** Repurposing successful content into different formats extends its lifecycle and broadens its reach across various platforms.

By integrating each stage of the content creation process, businesses can enhance efficiency while maintaining creativity. Start by selecting one tool that aligns your current challenges or goals, explore its features, and integrate it into your workflow. With a flexible approach tailored to your unique needs, AI can revolutionize your content creation strategy and help you achieve exceptional results.

Be aware of AI in content creation

These tools make advanced content creation accessible to everyone, regardless of technical expertise, but they need the human first step and guidance. By integrating such technologies into workflows, creators can produce high-quality content efficiently and effectively.

While it provides various benefits, it also has limitations that include potential biases in algorithms, lack of emotional intelligence, and the risk of over-reliance on technology. These factors can lead to ethical concerns, inaccuracies, and a diminished human touch in decision-making processes. Acknowledging these limitations is crucial for responsible AI usage, ensuring that it complements human capabilities rather than replacing them.

Benefits:

- **Efficiency**: AI can perform repetitive tasks at a much faster pace than humans, ensuring accuracy and freeing up time for creators to focus on more complex and creative aspects of their work.

- **Consistency**: AI tools can maintain a uniform brand voice and quality across all content produced, ensuring that messaging remains coherent and aligned with brand values.

- **Personalization**: AI can analyze audience data to deliver customized experiences, tailoring content to meet the specific preferences and needs of different segments of the audience.

Limitations:

- **Creativity**: AI lacks the emotional intelligence and nuanced understanding that human creators possess, which can result in content that feels flat or impersonal like post may miss the mark by not including personal anecdotes or emotional depth that resonate with readers.

- **Bias in Data**: AI outputs can mirror the biases present in the data used for training, leading to skewed or unfair results. Content like advertisements generated by biased data may unintentionally favor certain demographics, perpetuating inequality.

- **Over-Reliance**: Relying too heavily on AI can diminish the authenticity of interactions and content and it may come across as impersonal, leading to a disconnection with customers.

By understanding these benefits and challenges, creators can effectively balance the use of AI's efficiency with the essential human elements that contribute to unique and engaging content.

This also reinforce ethical considerations is crucial when integrating AI into content creation processes. Transparency about AI usage and ensuring fairness in outputs are essential steps toward responsible implementation. Following guidelines can help keep content and creativity in line with ethical principles:

- **Fact-Checking**: It is essential to verify the information produced by AI systems by cross-referencing it with credible and reliable sources. This process ensures that the data provided is accurate and trustworthy, reducing the risk of disseminating false information.

- **Bias Monitoring**: Regular assessments of AI outputs are necessary to identify and address any unintentional biases, stereotypes, or inaccuracies that may arise. This involves analyzing the results for fairness and representation, ensuring that the AI does not perpetuate harmful narratives or discrimination.

- **Human Oversight:** It is crucial to maintain a balance between automated processes and human intervention. Human oversight allows for critical evaluation of AI-generated content, ensuring that decisions made by AI align with ethical standards and societal values. This collaboration enhances the overall reliability and accountability of AI systems.

AI serves as a collaborative partner rather than a substitute for human creativity, enhancing both productivity and innovation. By adopting this perspective, creators can achieve greater efficiency and engagement in their work.

Utilize AI for preliminary tasks such as drafting content or analyzing data. However, it is crucial to refine and personalize the outputs to ensure they resonate with your unique voice and style. Maintaining authenticity by regularly interacting with your audience on a personal level helps to foster genuine connections and trust. If an AI tool is used to generate automated replies for social media interactions, it is beneficial to complement these automated messages with personalized responses or voice notes. This strategy not only enhances engagement but also strengthens the relationship with your audience.

Stay informed and continuously seek out and learn about new AI tools that can enhance your workflows. This proactive approach allows you to integrate the latest advancements into your creative process.

Integrating AI into content creation

We previously reviewed the process of integrating AI into business, its complexities and contributions for greater efficiency and results. For content creation, it is a similar integration process that we will review below with its particularities.

In the fast-paced world of digital content creation, professionals often find themselves bogged down by repetitive and time-consuming tasks. These responsibilities can stifle creativity and limit the time available for crafting impactful stories that resonate with audiences.

By integrating artificial intelligence into workflows, content creators can streamline their processes, unleash their creativity, and achieve greater efficiency. This guide provides a clear roadmap to adopt AI in content creation, addressing challenges, and leveraging best practices for success.

1. **Set Clear Objectives:** Before implementing AI tools, define specific goals such as improving efficiency, enhancing content quality, or boosting audience engagement. Some could be focusing on using AI-powered to schedule or automate posting across multiple platforms, or to free up time for strategic content planning and storytelling.

2. **Identifying Opportunities:** Evaluate current workflows and identify tasks that can benefit from automation. This ensures that AI adds the most value to the content creation process. Analyze your content creation process to pinpoint repetitive, time-consuming, or error-prone tasks. Examples include keyword research, trend analysis, initial content drafting, and scheduling social media posts.

3. **Recognize Automation Potential:** Tasks like data analysis and trend identification are ideal candidates for automation. For instance, instead of manually looking through search engine results for keywords, AI tools can generate keyword suggestions based on real-time trends.

4. **Prepare for Change:** By understanding which areas of your workflow can benefit from automation, you set the stage for a smoother transition to AI-powered processes. AI should complement human creativity rather than replace it.

   While AI excels at data analysis and pattern recognition, human intuition is crucial for interpreting insights and crafting compelling narratives. Encourage a collaborative approach where humans focus on innovation and storytelling and AI handles data-intensive tasks like trend analysis or performance tracking.

   By investing in training sessions and encouraging experimentation you can create a collaborative and innovative culture where team members feel comfortable with new tools and features, fostering innovation in content creation.

5. **Selecting and Implementing AI Tools:** Choosing the right AI tools is critical to addressing specific workflow challenges. A phased implementation ensures a seamless transition. Identify AI tools designed to address your specific challenges. For example, using platforms for content optimization or for social media scheduling.

6. **Uphold Data Security and Ethical Standards:** Maintaining strict data security and ethical practices is non-negotiable. Ensure that AI tools comply with data protection regulations, ethical guidelines regarding user privacy and consent are followed and transparency is maintained by clearly communicating when AI is involved in interactions with audiences.

7. **Start Small with Pilot Tests:** Implement selected AI tools on a smaller scale within your workflow. For instance, trial an AI-powered tool for generating blog outlines or automating analytics reports. This way you can look into different tools and find the ones that better manage your needs.

8. **Monitor and Evaluate Performance:** Gather feedback from your team on the usability and effectiveness of these tools. Use this feedback to refine your approach and ensure the tools meet your objectives. Embrace Continuous Improvement, AI technologies are constantly evolving. Regularly assess their performance and adapt strategies to stay ahead of industry trends. Some of these actions are to monitor user engagement metrics influenced by AI-generated content or adjust workflows based on new capabilities offered by updated AI tools.

Addressing Challenges in AI Integration

Integrating AI into content workflows presents several unique challenges that organizations must navigate. These challenges may include issues related to data quality, the need for specialized skills, resistance to change from team members, and the potential for bias in AI algorithms.

To address these obstacles, proactive solutions can be implemented. These may involve investing in training for staff to enhance their understanding of AI tools, establishing clear guidelines for data usage, and continuously monitoring AI outputs to ensure fairness and accuracy. By being aware of the next bullet points, organizations can effectively control AI to boost their content creation processes while minimizing potential pitfalls.

- **Integration Complexity:** Integrating AI tools into existing systems can be time-consuming. Prioritize tools with robust APIs and seamless integration capabilities. Choose platforms that align with your current infrastructure to simplify the process.

- **Cost Considerations:** The upfront investment in AI technologies can be challenging for smaller teams or organizations with limited budgets. Start with affordable AI solutions or trial subscriptions to evaluate potential returns on investment (ROI). Scale up gradually based on demonstrated productivity gains, cost savings from automation, and enhanced content quality.

- **Performance Monitoring:** Evaluating the impact of AI-driven tasks can be challenging due to a lack of clear benchmarks or metrics. Establish tailored key performance indicators (KPIs) such as accuracy rates in content generation or efficiency gains from automation. Regularly review performance data to refine strategies and maximize benefits.

Content Personalization and Audience Engagement

In today's rapidly changing digital environment, businesses face the challenge of constantly evolving their strategies to effectively connect with their target audiences. Artificial Intelligence has emerged as a groundbreaking tool that can significantly enhance this connection. By utilizing AI technologies, companies can create personalized content tailored to the preferences and behaviors of specific audience segments. This level of customization not only improves audience engagement but also contributes to overall business growth.

This chapter will delve into the transformative impact of AI on content strategies. It will explore various practical applications of AI in content creation, distribution, and analysis, highlighting how businesses can leverage these technologies to optimize their marketing efforts. Through these insights, teams gain a deeper understanding of the potential of AI in enhancing audience engagement and driving business success.

AI-powered analytics tools provide invaluable insights by analyzing vast amounts of data, such as demographic information, online behavior, and engagement patterns. These insights enable businesses to create personalized messages that resonate with specific audience groups.

Tailoring content to meet the unique needs of different audience segments is crucial for building meaningful connections. AI offers advanced instruments to achieve this on a scale.

1) **Audience Segmentation:** AI tools like Google Analytics and Adobe Analytics can identify distinct audience segments based on factors such as demographic, purchasing behavior, and browsing history. Develop tailored marketing campaigns for each segment to optimize engagement.

2) **Content Preferences:** AI can reveal trends, such as younger audiences preferring dynamic social media campaigns while older audiences respond better to email newsletters with exclusive offers.

3) **Individualized experience:** AI recommendation systems analyze user data, such as purchase history or viewing habits, to predict preferences and suggest relevant content. This approach not only enhances user satisfaction but also fosters repeat visits and purchases. Use machine learning algorithms to predict user preferences and optimize suggestions. Enhance customer retention by providing a smooth, personalized experience.

4) **Content Optimization**: AI tools can optimize content creation processes by analyzing performance data and identifying opportunities for improvement. They offer actionable recommendations to improve content quality and search engine visibility. These tools analyze top-performing content, suggest relevant keywords, provide insights into audience preferences, anticipate trends, leverage sentiment analysis to gauge audience emotions and refine messaging.

5) **Interactive Engagement:** Interactive AI technologies can create immersive experiences that deepen audience engagement. AI-powered chatbots, augmented reality (AR), and virtual reality (VR) are reshaping how businesses interact with their audiences. These tools

provide instant responses, personalized recommendations, and engaging experiences. Integrated chatbots into websites or apps to provide 24/7 customer support or use AR or VR technologies for interactive product demonstrations or storytelling.

Staying ahead of emerging trends is crucial for businesses to maintain their competitive edge. In a rapidly changing landscape, organizations must continuously monitor and adapt to new developments in technology, consumer behavior, and market dynamics. This proactive approach allows businesses to identify opportunities for innovation, improve their products and services, and respond effectively to shifts in demand. By being aware of trends, companies can also anticipate challenges and mitigate risks, ensuring long-term sustainability and growth in an ever-evolving environment.

Some of the future trends in AI content strategies that we can expect are hyper-personalization, voice and visual search optimization, AR and VR integration refinement and upgraded AI content generation.

Measuring Impact

To effectively assess the impact of AI-driven strategies, it is essential to establish specific metrics that can quantify performance and outcomes. These metrics should encompass various aspects such as accuracy, efficiency, user engagement, and return on investment. Continuous analysis is crucial, as it allows for real-time monitoring and adjustments to strategies based on performance data. This iterative process ensures that AI implementations remain aligned with organizational goals and can adapt to changing circumstances or new insights. Regular reviews and updates to the metrics and analysis methods will further enhance the understanding of AI effectiveness over time.

It is crucial to define these metrics in alignment with the business objectives and engagement goals to ensure that the evaluation of success is relevant and meaningful. The definition of the KPIs must be clear and specific, be based on trustful data and advance analysis, and consider audience sentiment through comments, reviews, and social media. Key metrics to consider include:

- **Click-Through Rates (CTR)**: This metric indicates the percentage of users who click on a specific link compared to the total number of users who view the content. A higher CTR suggests that the content is engaging and relevant to the audience.

- **Time Spent on Page**: This measures the average duration that users spend on a webpage. Longer time spent on a page can indicate that the content is engaging and holds the audience's attention.

- **Social Shares**: This metric tracks how often content is shared across social media platforms. A high number of shares can reflect the content's appeal and its potential to reach a wider audience.

- **Conversion Rates**: This measures the percentage of users who take a desired action after engaging with the content, such as making a purchase or signing up for a newsletter. High conversion rates are indicative of effective content that drives user action.

By continuously analyzing these metrics, organizations can gain valuable insights into content performance and make informed decisions to optimize their AI-driven strategies for better engagement and success.

Iterative refinement is essential for keeping content strategies relevant and effective. By consistently gathering audience feedback and analyzing engagement patterns, businesses can dynamically adjust their strategies. This ongoing process ensures that the content stays in tune with audience preferences and current market trends. This can be reached by collecting qualitative feedback through surveys or direct interactions, segmenting your audience further using advanced profiling tools and exploring new content formats or topics based on data-driven insights.

AI represents a paradigm shift in how businesses engage with their audiences. By harnessing its capabilities to tailor content, optimize strategies, and embrace emerging trends, companies can achieve unparalleled levels of relevance and effectiveness. As the digital landscape continues to evolve, staying informed about advancements in AI will empower businesses to exceed audience expectations and drive sustained growth.

By integrating these insights into your content strategy, you can unlock new possibilities for innovation and success. The journey toward mastering AI-powered content creation depends on the strategy to embrace the potential, stay curious, and let AI guide your path to excellence. Remember that AI gives countless tools, but the real creation is on you and your team's creativity to reach your audience.

Chapter 6

Ensuring the Trustworthiness of AI Solutions

Artificial Intelligence has revolutionized the way businesses operate, offering automation and efficiency at unprecedented levels. The integration of AI technologies into various sectors has transformed traditional processes, enabling organizations to streamline operations, enhance productivity, and improve decision-making. From customer service chatbots to advanced data analytics, AI applications are becoming increasingly prevalent, allowing businesses to gain a competitive edge in the market.

However, deploying AI solutions without thorough testing can lead to significant risks. These risks include inaccurate outputs, which can result in poor decision-making and financial losses. For instance, if an AI system used for financial forecasting produces erroneous predictions, it could lead to misguided investments or budget allocations. Additionally, reputational damage can occur if customers or stakeholders perceive the AI's performance as unreliable or biased. In some cases, the deployment of flawed AI systems can even lead to legal consequences, particularly if they violate regulations or fail to comply with ethical standards.

On the other hand, the rapid rise of AI tools, particularly generative AI, and deep learning models, enable the creation of highly realistic outputs, including deep-fake images and fabricated text, which can be utilized for entertainment, marketing, and other creative endeavors where one major issue is the potential for misinformation. The ability of AI to generate convincing but false content can lead to the spread of false narratives, impacting public opinion and trust. This is particularly concerning in contexts such as news media and social platforms, where the line between reality and fabrication can become blurred.

Additionally, the lack of human qualities in AI, such as empathy and common sense, poses ethical dilemmas. AI systems may not fully understand the nuances of human emotions or moral considerations, leading to decisions that could be harmful or inappropriate in sensitive situations. This raises questions about accountability, especially when AI-generated content causes harm or perpetuates bias.

Furthermore, the misuse of AI technologies is a significant risk. Individuals or groups may exploit these tools for malicious purposes, such as creating misleading propaganda or engaging in identity theft through deepfakes. The potential for abuse necessitates a careful examination of the ethical frameworks and regulations surrounding AI development and deployment.

Likewise, AI systems, while powerful and capable of processing vast amounts of information, are fallible and can exhibit significant limitations. One common issue that arises in the realm of artificial intelligence is the occurrence of "hallucinations." This term refers to instances where AI models generate outputs that are incorrect, unreasonable, or entirely fabricated. These hallucinations can manifest in various forms, from simple genuine inaccuracies to more complex and misleading information.

For instance, consider an AI-powered accounting chatbot designed to provide users with tax information. If this chatbot were to incorrectly advise users with the wrong indications, forms or taxes timelines, the implications could be horrible. Such an error not only undermines the credibility of the AI system but also poses serious risks to users from banking credibility, penalties, interest charges, and, in extreme cases, jail time. The potential for harm is particularly disturbing in critical scenarios where accurate information is vital, such as in healthcare, legal advice, or emergency response situations.

While these errors may seem absurd or exaggerated, they serve as a stark reminder of the inherent risks associated with relying on untested or inadequately validated AI systems. The consequences of these hallucinations can range from minor misunderstandings to life-threatening situations, emphasizing the need for caution and thorough oversight when integrating AI technologies into sensitive areas of society. As AI continues to evolve and become more integrated into our daily lives, it is crucial to address these challenges and ensure that robust mechanisms are in place to mitigate the risks associated with AI-generated misinformation.

The consequences of such inaccuracies can range from minor inconveniences to severe outcomes, such as providing incorrect allergy-related information to users with life-threatening conditions. Businesses must recognize that users often perceive AI systems as highly trustworthy, and errors can erode customer confidence and damage brand reputation.

Key Considerations for AI Use:

- **Accuracy vs. Creativity:** AI models excel at generating creative content but may "hallucinate" or fabricate details. Double-check facts and sources when using AI for critical tasks.

- **Ethical Concerns:** AI can perpetuate harm, such as deepfake frauds or inappropriate emotional responses. Always assess the potential consequences of its application.

- **Fact-Checking Tools:** Utilize platforms like Snopes, Deepfake Detector, or GPT-Zero to verify content authenticity.

- **Judgment and Skepticism:** Be vigilant about the origin of information and question its credibility.

AI is a tool, not a substitute for human expertise. Its effectiveness depends on how it is used and monitored. By staying informed and skeptical, individuals and businesses can harness its potential while minimizing risks.

Testing is Crucial

Testing is a critical component in the development of AI solutions, as it guarantees that these systems not only fulfill their intended requirements but also operate reliably over time. This process involves a series of evaluations and assessments designed to identify any potential issues or inconsistencies in the AI's performance. By rigorously testing AI applications, developers can ensure that they function consistently, providing users with a dependable experience.

Moreover, robust testing is essential for maintaining the integrity of AI solutions, especially when they are subjected to external changes. For instance, updates to third-party tools or platforms that the AI relies on can introduce unforeseen challenges. Through comprehensive testing, developers can anticipate these changes and adapt their solutions, accordingly, ensuring that the AI remains resilient and effective.

Whether the project at hand is a straightforward automation tool designed to streamline specific tasks or a sophisticated chatbot capable of engaging in complex conversations, the importance of testing cannot be overstated. It serves as a safeguard against potential risks, allowing developers to identify and rectify issues before they impact end-users. This proactive approach not only enhances the functionality of the AI but also contributes to a seamless user experience, fostering trust and satisfaction among users.

Thorough testing is indispensable in the AI development lifecycle. It not only verifies that the solutions meet their design specifications but also ensures that they can withstand external pressures and continue to deliver value to users. By prioritizing testing, developers can create AI systems that are not only innovative but also reliable and user-friendly.

For example, consider a website that collects email addresses for a newsletter. Basic testing would involve verifying that only valid email addresses are accepted and ensuring the data is added correctly to the mailing list. As solutions grow in complexity, testing becomes even more critical to identify potential vulnerabilities and ensure reliability.

Strategies for Thorough Testing

When developing and deploying an AI solution, it is crucial to follow a structured approach to ensure that the system functions as intended and meets the desired objectives. Here are the detailed steps to consider:

1. **Define Objectives**: Clearly outline the goals of the AI solution. What problem is it solving? What are the success metrics? This step is essential for guiding the development process.

2. **Data Collection**: Gather relevant data that will be used to train the AI model. Ensure that the data is diverse, representative, and of high quality to avoid biases and inaccuracies in the model's predictions.

3. **Data Preprocessing**: Clean and preprocess the data to make it suitable for training. This may involve handling missing values, normalizing data, and transforming categorical variables into numerical formats.

4. **Model Selection**: Choose the appropriate AI model or algorithm based on the problem type (e.g., classification, regression, clustering). Consider factors such as complexity, interpretability, and performance.

5. **Training the Model**: Split the data into training and validation sets. Train the model using the training set while tuning hyperparameters to optimize performance. Use the validation set to evaluate the model's effectiveness.

6. **Testing and Evaluation**: After training, test the model on a separate test dataset to assess its performance. Use metrics such as accuracy, precision, recall, and F1 score to evaluate how well the model performs.

7. **Deployment**: Once the model is validated and performs satisfactorily, deploy it into a production environment. This may involve integrating the model into existing systems or creating a new application.

8. **Monitoring and Maintenance**: Continuously monitor the AI solution's performance in the real world. Collect feedback and data to identify any issues or areas for improvement. Regularly update the model as new data becomes available to maintain its accuracy and relevance.

9. **Ethical Considerations**: Throughout the development and deployment process, consider the ethical implications of the AI solution. Ensure that it adheres to guidelines for fairness, accountability, and transparency.

10. **User Training and Support**: Provide training and support for users who will interact with the AI solution. Ensure they understand how to use it effectively and are aware of its limitations.

By following these steps, you can develop and deploy an AI solution that not only functions as intended but also delivers value and meets the needs of its users.

Example Process for Resolving Issues

If an issue arises during testing, follow this structured approach:

1. **Assess the Impact:** Determine how the issue affects the overall functionality and user experience.

2. **Identify the Root Cause:** Pinpoint the underlying problem to address it effectively.

3. **Implement a Fix:** Make necessary adjustments to resolve the issue.

4. **Re-Test Thoroughly:** Verify that the fix works across multiple scenarios to prevent recurrence.

5. **Document the Solution:** Record the problem and its resolution for future reference.

6. **Continuous Improvement:** Always be looking and ready for new issues and updates.

Even after thorough testing, mistakes can occasionally slip through the cracks, despite the best efforts of teams to ensure quality and accuracy. This is a common occurrence in many fields, including software development, product design, and even in service-oriented industries. When such errors are identified, it is crucial to focus on resolving the issue promptly. This means not only addressing the immediate problem but also understanding the root cause to prevent similar mistakes in the future.

Maintaining transparency with stakeholders during this process is essential. Stakeholders can include team members, management, clients, and customers who rely on the product or service. By communicating openly about the issue, the steps being taken to resolve it, and the expected timeline for resolution, trust can be preserved.

Stakeholders appreciate honesty and are more likely to remain supportive when they feel informed and involved.

It is important to remember that perfection is not always achievable in any endeavor. Mistakes are a natural part of the learning and development process. However, a commitment to continuous improvement is what truly fosters trust and reliability. By demonstrating a proactive approach to problem-solving and a willingness to learn from errors, organizations can build a reputation for resilience and accountability. This not only enhances relationships with stakeholders but also contributes to a culture of excellence and innovation within the team.

Safeguarding Data and compliance

As businesses continue to adopt AI and data-driven technologies, safeguarding personal data remains a critical legal and ethical responsibility. The integration of artificial intelligence into various sectors has revolutionized operations, enhancing efficiency and decision-making processes. However, this rapid advancement also raises significant concerns regarding the privacy and security of individuals' personal information.

Organizations must navigate a complex landscape of regulations, such as the General Data Protection Regulation (GDPR) in Europe and the California Consumer Privacy Act (CCPA) in the United States, which impose strict guidelines on how personal data is collected, stored, and utilized. Failure to comply with these regulations can result in severe penalties and damage to a company's reputation.

Moreover, ethical considerations come into play as businesses must ensure that their AI systems are designed to respect user privacy and avoid biases that could lead to discrimination. This involves implementing robust data protection measures, conducting regular audits, and fostering a culture of transparency and accountability.

As the reliance on AI and data analytics grows, so does the imperative for businesses to prioritize the protection of personal data, balancing innovation with the fundamental rights of individuals.

U.S. Data Privacy Framework

In the United States, while there is no single federal data protection law yet (2024), a patchwork of state and sector-specific legislation has emerged, alongside federal guidance, to address privacy and data security concerns. Here we provide an overview of key U.S. data protection laws and actionable steps for businesses to ensure compliance in an AI-driven landscape.

Please note that this information refers to current regulations (2024) and is constantly changing as technology advances. It is your duty to keep yourselves up to date and in order with the latest legislation that is published.

The U.S. approach to data privacy is characterized by a sectoral and state-driven framework, meaning that regulations can vary significantly depending on the industry and the state in which a business operates. This decentralized model has led to a patchwork of laws that businesses must navigate to ensure compliance. In recent years, there have been significant developments in this area, reflecting growing concerns about consumer privacy and data security.

Businesses operating in the U.S. should focus on several key laws and principles that govern data privacy:

— **The California Consumer Privacy Act (CCPA) / California Privacy Rights Act (CPRA)**: This landmark legislation grants California residents specific rights regarding their personal information, including the right to know what data is being collected, the right to delete personal data, and the right to opt-out of the sale of their data. The CCPA, effective January 1, 2023, expands these rights and creates a dedicated enforcement agency and has set a precedent for other states considering similar laws.

Other states have enacted similar legislation, with varying requirements, like Virginia (Virginia Consumer Data Protection Act), Colorado (Colorado Privacy Act), Connecticut (Connecticut Data Privacy Act), and Utah (Utah Consumer Privacy Act).

Overall, many states have enacted their own data privacy laws, which can include additional requirements for data breach notifications, consumer rights, and data protection measures. Businesses must stay informed about the specific regulations in each state where they operate.

- **The Health Insurance Portability and Accountability Act (HIPAA):** For businesses in the healthcare sector, HIPAA establishes federal standards for the protection of health information. It mandates safeguards to ensure the confidentiality, integrity, and security of protected health information (PHI).

- **The Gramm-Leach-Bliley Act (GLBA):** This federal law applies to financial institutions and requires them to explain their information-sharing practices to their customers and to safeguard sensitive data.

- **The Children's Online Privacy Protection Act (COPPA):** This federal law imposes certain requirements on services directed to children under 13 years of age, including obtaining verifiable parental consent before collecting personal information from children.

- **General Data Protection Regulation (GDPR) Considerations:** While GDPR is a European regulation, it has implications for U.S.

businesses that handle the personal data of EU citizens. Compliance with GDPR can be complex and requires a thorough understanding of its principles, including data minimization, purpose limitation, and the rights of data subjects.

While a comprehensive federal privacy law remains under debate in Congress, recent bipartisan proposals, such as the American Data Privacy Protection Act (ADPPA) signals potential progress toward unified national standards.

To navigate this complex regulatory environment, businesses should adhere to these core principles:

- **Transparency:** Clearly disclose data collection and processing practices in privacy policies.

- **Consent and Opt-Out Mechanisms:** Provide users with mechanisms to opt out of data sales or processing where required by law.

- **Data Minimization:** Limit data collection to what is necessary for specific business purposes.

- **Security Measures:** Implement robust data security practices to protect against breaches.

- **Consumer Rights:** Facilitate consumer requests for access, deletion, or correction of their personal data in compliance with applicable state laws.

Non-compliance with U.S. privacy laws can lead to severe consequences for businesses, including hefty financial penalties, legal actions, and damage to their reputation in the marketplace. The California Consumer Privacy Act (CCPA) and its successor, the California Privacy Rights Act (CPRA), impose strict regulations on how businesses handle personal data. Under these laws, companies that are found to have intentionally violated consumer privacy rights can face fines that reach as high as $7,500 for each intentional violation. This means that if a business repeatedly fails to comply with the regulations, the cumulative fines can escalate quickly, resulting in significant financial burdens.

In addition to state-level penalties, businesses must also be aware of federal regulations enforced by the Federal Trade Commission (FTC). The FTC has the authority to act against companies that engage in unfair or deceptive practices related to consumer privacy. These enforcement actions can result in substantial financial penalties, which can vary based on the severity of the violation and the number of affected consumers. Furthermore, the reputational damage that accompanies such legal actions can have long-lasting effects on a business's relationship with its customers, potentially leading to a loss of trust and a decline in customer loyalty.

Overall, the implications of non-compliance with privacy laws are far-reaching, making it essential for businesses to prioritize adherence to these regulations to avoid financial repercussions and maintain their reputation in an increasingly privacy-conscious market.

The U.S. data privacy landscape is evolving, and businesses must remain vigilant in understanding and complying with the various laws and regulations that apply to their operations. By focusing on these key laws and principles, businesses can better protect consumer data and mitigate the risks associated with data privacy violations.

Understanding GDPR

In regions like the European Union (EU) and the United Kingdom (UK), compliance with regulations such as the General Data Protection Regulation (GDPR) is essential for legal and ethical operations. It is a comprehensive data protection law that was enacted in the European Union (EU) to enhance individuals' control over their personal data and to unify data protection regulations across Europe. It aims to protect the privacy and personal information of EU citizens and residents, ensuring that their data is handled with care and respect.

The regulation consists of numerous provisions, but businesses can focus on several core principles to ensure compliance:

- **Consent is Mandatory:** Under GDPR, individuals must provide explicit consent for their personal data to be processed. This means that businesses cannot assume consent through inactivity or pre-checked boxes; instead, individuals must actively opt-in to data processing activities. This principle emphasizes the importance of transparency and informed decision-making.

- **Right to Withdraw Consent:** GDPR grants users the right to withdraw their consent at any time. If an individual decides they no longer want their personal data to be processed, they can request its deletion. Organizations are required to comply with such requests within one month, although there are specific exceptions that may apply in certain situations.

- **Access Rights:** Individuals have the right to access their personal data held by organizations. They can request a copy of their data, and organizations must provide this information within one month. In some cases, this timeframe may be extended to two months if the request is complex or if the organization receives numerous requests.

- **Legitimate Processing:** Data processing must be conducted for lawful purposes. This includes fulfilling contractual obligations, complying with legal requirements, protecting vital interests, performing tasks carried out in the public interest, or pursuing legitimate interests, provided these do not override the rights and freedoms of individuals.

- **Accuracy Obligation:** Organizations are responsible for ensuring that the personal data they hold is accurate and up to date. This means that businesses must take reasonable steps to rectify any inaccuracies in the data they process and ensure that outdated information is removed.

Non-compliance with the General Data Protection Regulation (GDPR) can lead to significant repercussions for organizations that fail to adhere to their stringent requirements. The GDPR, which came into effect on May 25, 2018, is a comprehensive data protection law in the European Union that aims to enhance individuals' control over their personal data and to unify data protection regulations across the EU member states.

One of the most severe consequences of non-compliance is the imposition of hefty financial penalties. Organizations found in violation of the GDPR can face fines that amount to up to 4% of their total annual global turnover or €20 million, whichever is greater. This means that for large corporations with substantial revenues, the fines can be astronomical, potentially reaching hundreds of millions of euros.

In addition to financial penalties, non-compliance can also lead to reputational damage, loss of customer trust, and legal actions from affected individuals or regulatory bodies. Organizations may also be required to implement corrective measures, which can incur additional costs and operational disruptions.

It is crucial for businesses operating within the EU or handling the personal data of EU citizens to ensure they are fully compliant with GDPR regulations to avoid these severe penalties and maintain their reputation in the marketplace.

To simplify adherence to GDPR requirements, businesses should implement the following best practices:

- **Record Consent Details:** It is crucial for organizations to maintain detailed records of when and how individuals provided their consent for data processing. This includes documenting the specific terms and conditions that were presented to individuals at the time of consent. Keeping a copy or version number of these documents can serve as a reference in case of audits or inquiries.

- **Track Collected Data:** Businesses should create a comprehensive log of all personal data being collected and processed. This log should include details such as names, addresses, phone numbers, and any other relevant information. Even simple documentation can help maintain transparency and accountability regarding data handling practices.

- **Store Data Locally:** Organizations should ensure that personal data is stored within compliant regions, such as the EU or UK, especially when utilizing cloud providers or online tools. Many cloud service providers offer location-specific storage options, which can help businesses comply with GDPR requirements regarding data residency.

- **Prepare for Breaches:** It is essential for organizations to develop a robust response plan outlining the steps to take in the event of a data breach. This plan should include procedures for notifying affected individuals and regulatory authorities promptly, as well as measures to mitigate the impact of the breach and prevent future occurrences.

By following these principles and best practices, businesses can work towards achieving compliance with GDPR, thereby protecting the personal data of individuals, and fostering trust in their data handling practices.

Beyond compliance with specific laws, businesses should adopt robust data security practices to protect personal information from breaches and unauthorized access. This includes implementing encryption, conducting regular security audits, and training employees on data protection protocols.

As the regulatory landscape continues to evolve, businesses must stay informed about legislative changes at local and international levels. Proactively adopting privacy-by-design principles and maintaining a robust compliance framework will be essential for operating responsibly in an AI-driven world.

Data Protection in AI Applications

AI systems often require significant amounts of data for training and operation, as the effectiveness of these systems largely depends on the quality and quantity of the data they are exposed to. This data can include a wide range of information, from user interactions and preferences to more sensitive personal information. Therefore, it is crucial for businesses and organizations to understand how third-party AI service providers handle this data to avoid compliance risks and potential legal issues.

For instance, some AI service providers may utilize customer data to train their models, which raises concerns about data privacy and security. If sensitive information is inadvertently included in the training data, it could lead to that information being revealed in future outputs generated by the AI. This scenario poses a significant risk, especially in industries that handle confidential or personal data, such as healthcare, finance, and legal services.

On the other hand, some providers, such as Amazon Web Services (AWS), have implemented strict measures to ensure that customer data remains private and secure. AWS guarantees that customer data does not leave their networks during AI processing, thereby minimizing the risk of data breaches and unauthorized access. This level of commitment to data privacy is essential for businesses that prioritize the protection of their customers' information.

Given these varying approaches to data handling, businesses must carefully review service agreements and policies before utilizing AI tools to process personal data. This due diligence is vital to ensure alignment with both legal regulations' requirements and the organization's values regarding data privacy and ethical use of technology. By understanding the data practices of AI service providers, businesses can make informed decisions that safeguard their data and maintain compliance with relevant regulations.

Ethical Navigation in the Age of AI

Emerging technologies like AI can offer remarkable benefits but also present significant risks, particularly when they perpetuate biases or cause harm. Businesses must take responsibility for ensuring their technologies are fair, accurate, and ethical while balancing the need for innovation.

In particular, a company's ethical responsibilities extend beyond simply following laws; they must also consider their broader impact on society. This includes areas like sustainability, inclusion, and diversity, often referred to as Environmental, Social and Governance (ESG) principles.

Ethics in business refers to acting in a morally responsible way while considering values and principles when making decisions. However, the profit motive can sometimes conflict with ethical decision-making. Just as sports require referees to ensure fair play, businesses need ethical frameworks to guide their practices.

One of the challenges with emerging technologies is that regulation often comes behind innovation. For example, while social media has existed for decades, its impact on mental health is only now being fully understood and addressed. Similarly, AI tools can have far-reaching consequences before laws catch up to govern their use effectively.

Managing technology in an unregulated environment involves questioning the intentions behind new technologies, the benefits and accountability of the owner. Users and developers must stay informed about evolving regulations and societal discussions and proactively address potential risks before external regulations require it.

To effectively navigate new technologies, individuals and businesses must cultivate ethical awareness by questioning how tools are designed and used by recognizing that cultural differences influence perceptions of what is right or wrong. This global perspective is crucial as technologies often have a wide-reaching impact across diverse communities.

While no technology is inherently good or bad, its impact depends on how it is used. Biases present in society can manifest in technology unless actively addressed. To navigate technology ethically business and individual must develop critical thinking to validate AI accuracy with reliable sources. We all need to understand the limitations, particularly in areas requiring empathy or common sense, and focus on soft skills like empathy, creativity, and lateral thinking that AI cannot replicate effectively.

By establishing ethical safeguards and anticipating potential challenges, organizations can foster trust and accountability for the core principles of technology management:
- Evaluate societal and individual impacts of new tools.
- Intervene promptly to mitigate harm or inequity.
- Implement protective measures to ensure user safety.
- Anticipate and address potential risks proactively.

In summary, by embracing rigorous testing practices and adhering to data protection regulations, businesses can harness the full potential of artificial intelligence while maintaining trust and compliance with legal and ethical standards. This commitment to thorough testing ensures that AI systems are not only effective but also safe and reliable, minimizing the likelihood of errors or unintended consequences that could arise from their deployment.

Moreover, by following stringent data protection regulations, organizations can safeguard sensitive information, thereby fostering a culture of transparency and accountability. This is particularly crucial in an era where data breaches and privacy concerns are prevalent, as consumers are increasingly aware of their rights and the importance of data security.

These proactive measures not only mitigate risks associated with AI implementation but also position organizations as responsible stewards of technology in an increasingly digital world. By demonstrating a commitment to ethical practices and compliance, businesses can build and maintain trust with their customers, stakeholders, and the broader community. This trust is essential for long-term success, as it encourages customer loyalty and enhances the organization's reputation in the marketplace.

Chapter 7

Workplace Dynamics and AI

Artificial Intelligence continues to reshape the modern workplace, bringing both opportunities and challenges for employers and employees alike. The integration of AI technologies into various sectors has led to significant transformations in how work is conducted, enhancing efficiency and productivity while also introducing complexities that must be addressed. Understanding its potential, limitations, and ethical implications is crucial for leveraging its benefits while mitigating associated risks.

For employers, AI can streamline operations, reduce costs, and improve decision-making processes through data analysis and predictive modeling. However, the implementation of AI also raises concerns about the myth of job displacement and that automation may replace certain roles, leading to workforce reductions. Employers must navigate these challenges by investing in employee retraining and upskilling programs to ensure that their workforce can adapt to new technologies and remain competitive in an evolving job market.

On the other hand, employees face a dual-edged blade with the rise of AI. While AI can enhance their work experience by automating mundane tasks and providing valuable insights, it also poses the risk of job insecurity and the need for continuous learning. Employees must be proactive in developing their skills and embracing lifelong learning to thrive in an AI-driven environment.

So, there is a dual perspective of AI in the workplace offering practical strategies for navigating this evolving landscape and both must emphasize in the importance of collaboration between management and staff to create a culture of innovation and adaptability. By fostering open communication and involving employees in the AI integration process, organizations can build trust and ensure a smoother transition to a more automated workplace.

Additionally, ethical considerations surrounding AI, such as data privacy, bias in algorithms, and the impact on employee well-being, must be addressed. Organizations should establish clear guidelines and policies to govern the use of AI, ensuring that it aligns with their values and promotes a fair and inclusive work environment.

By understanding the implications of AI and adopting a proactive approach through strategic planning, employers and employees can work together to harness the potential of this technology while minimizing its risks.

The employer's perspective

Employers are increasingly turning to AI tools to enhance efficiency, monitor productivity, and support decision-making. These advanced technologies offer a range of capabilities, from automating routine tasks to providing data-driven insights that can inform strategic planning. For instance, AI can analyze vast amounts of data in real-time, allowing organizations to identify trends and make informed decisions quickly. Additionally, AI tools can streamline workflows, reduce human error, and free up employees to focus on more complex and creative tasks, ultimately leading to increased productivity and innovation.

However, the adoption of AI comes with significant responsibilities. Organizations must ensure ethical use of these technologies to avoid potential biases and discrimination that can arise from flawed algorithms or data sets. It is crucial for employers to implement transparent practices and maintain accountability in how AI systems are developed and deployed. This includes regularly auditing AI tools for fairness and accuracy, as well as providing training for employees on how to use these systems responsibly.

Moreover, maintaining trust within the organization is paramount. Employees may feel apprehensive about AI monitoring their productivity, fearing that it could lead to micromanagement or job insecurity. To address these concerns, employers should foster an open dialogue about the role of AI in the workplace, emphasizing its purpose as a tool for support rather than surveillance. By prioritizing ethical considerations and employee engagement, organizations can harness the benefits of AI while cultivating a positive and trusting work environment.

Key Benefits of AI for Employers

AI has the potential to revolutionize operations across various industries by automating repetitive tasks, analyzing vast datasets, and improving decision-making processes. This transformation can lead to increased efficiency, reduced operational costs, and enhanced productivity.

Overall, the integration of AI into various operational processes can lead to significant advancements and competitive advantages for organizations willing to embrace this technology.

Some notable applications of AI include:
- **Automation of Repetitive Tasks**
- **Data Analysis**
- **Improved Decision-Making**
- **Customer Service Enhancement**
- **Personalization**
- **Predictive Maintenance**
- **Fraud Detection**
- **Supply Chain Optimization**

Ethical Considerations for Employers

While AI offers significant benefits, its misuse can affect trust and create a negative work environment. This duality presents a challenge for employers who must carefully navigate the following concerns:
- **Data Privacy**
- **Bias and Discrimination**
- **Job Displacement**
- **Lack of Accountability**
- **Employee Engagement**
- **Change Management**

By addressing these concerns proactively, employers can harness the benefits of AI while fostering a positive and trusting work environment.

Practical Steps for Employers

To be responsible for implementing AI in the workplace, employers should:
- **Assess Needs and Objectives**
- **Engage Stakeholders**
- **Provide Training and Support**
- **Ensure Transparency**
- **Prioritize Ethics and Fairness**
- **Establish Clear Policies**
- **Monitor and Evaluate**
- **Foster a Culture of Innovation**

By following these steps, employers can effectively and responsibly integrate AI into their operations, maximizing benefits while minimizing potential risks.

The employee point of view

For employees, the integration of AI into the workplace presents both opportunities for growth and challenges related to privacy and job security. On one hand, allowing employees to focus on more strategic and creative aspects of their jobs leads to skill development and career advancement. But it also may feel uneasy about how their data is being used and monitored, leading to a potential loss of trust between workers and employers.

There is a looming fear of job displacement, as AI technologies can perform certain tasks more efficiently than humans, this creates a pressing need for employees to adapt to new roles and acquire new skills to remain relevant in an evolving job market. It is the employer's responsibility to transmit that AI is here as a tool to enhance their performance, not to replace them, as AI cannot function without them.

Embracing lifelong learning and being open to change will be crucial to thrive in an AI-driven workplace. Organizations, too, must prioritize transparency and ethical considerations in their use of AI to foster a supportive environment where employees feel secure and valued.

Key Benefits of AI for Employees

When used effectively, AI can empower employees by enhancing productivity and enabling skill development. Examples include:
- **Task Automation**
- **Skill Enhancement**
- **Work-Life Balance**

Concerns for Employees

Despite its benefits, employees must remain vigilant about potential downsides that can arise in the workplace. These downsides may include effects in both personal and work life, such as:
- **Stress due to heightened expectations**
- **Potential burnout from overwork due to over monitoring**
- **Risk of diminished work-life balance**
- **Workplace conflicts from miscommunication**
- **Loss of Privacy**
- **Job Displacement**
- **Dependence on Technology**

By staying informed and proactive, employees can navigate these challenges effectively while still reaping the rewards of their work environment, always working collaboratively with their team and leaders for success.

Practical Steps for Employees

To navigate the challenges of AI in the workplace, employees should keep in mind:
- **Adapt to Change**
- **Embrace Continuous Learning**
- **Developing Critical Thinking Skills**
- **Foster Collaboration with AI**
- **Communicate Openly**
- **Focus on Soft Skills**
- **Stay Ethical**

By following these strategies, employees can effectively navigate the challenges posed by AI in the workplace and position themselves for success in an increasingly automated environment.

Human Skills and AI Capabilities

As artificial intelligence continues to evolve and become more integrated into various workplaces, it is essential to prioritize the development and enhancement of human skills that are inherently unique and cannot be easily replicated by machines. These skills encompass a wide range of abilities and interpersonal communication necessary for building relationships, negotiating, and effectively conveying ideas and feedback.

Organizations that recognize the value of these skills and invest in their development will be better positioned to thrive in an automated world, as they will have a workforce capable of complementing and enhancing the capabilities of AI, rather than being replaced by it.

Key Human Skills to Develop

- **Emotional Intelligence:** Empathy, active listening, and interpersonal communication are essential for building strong relationships.

- **Critical Thinking:** The ability to analyze information objectively and make sound decisions remains irreplaceable.

- **Leadership:** Guiding teams through change and fostering collaboration will be paramount in navigating the AI era.

- **Adaptability:** Embracing change and learning new tools will help employees stay relevant in a dynamic environment.

Preparing for the Future of Work

The rapid evolution of AI technology necessitates proactive preparation for its impact on the workplace. As AI continues to advance at an unprecedented pace, it is crucial for organizations to anticipate the changes it will bring to job roles, workflows, and overall business operations.

Employers must invest in training and development programs, fostering a culture of continuous learning to remain competitive and relevant in a rapidly changing job market.

On the other hand, employees should take the initiative to improve and reskill themselves to enhance their employability and contribute meaningfully to their organizations'.

Collaboration between employers and employees is essential, as it creates a shared vision for the future of work that leverages the strengths of both human intelligence and artificial intelligence.

The Role of Human Rights in Shaping AI

Human rights principles provide a critical foundation for governing the use of AI in workplaces. These principles ensure that technological advancements do not come at the cost of fundamental freedoms and dignity.

Main Concerns:

- **Privacy and Data Security:** Individuals have the right to control their personal data. Businesses must ensure that employee data collected by AI systems is securely stored and not misused for profit or surveillance.

- **Freedom of Expression:** Employees should not face restrictions on their opinions due to AI-driven monitoring systems. For example, social media monitoring tools should not be used to penalize workers for expressing personal views outside the workplace.

- **Fair Labor Practices:** The hidden labor behind training AI systems must be acknowledged and regulated. Exploitative practices, such as underpaying workers for labeling harmful content, undermine basic labor rights.

- **Protection of Vulnerable Groups:** Children and other vulnerable populations are particularly at risk from generative AI technologies that blur the line between real and synthetic content. Businesses must take extra care to prevent harm in such cases.

Actionable Recommendations

For Employers:
- Invest in employee training programs.
- Collaborate with cross-functional teams.
- Ensure ethical implementation of AI tools.
- Regularly review policies and legal standards.

For Employees:
- Experiment with AI tools to discover their potential.

- Share insights about effective AI usage.
- Stay informed.

For Both:
- Promote a culture of transparency and open communication.
- Emphasize ethical considerations.
- Recognize the importance of balancing technological advancements with human-centric values.

AI has the potential to transform workplaces by enhancing efficiency, fostering innovation, and improving decision-making. However, its successful integration depends on responsible implementation, ethical considerations, and a commitment to preserving human values. By understanding both the opportunities and challenges of AI from employer and employee perspectives, organizations can create a balanced approach that benefits all stakeholders.

Appendix

TOOLS to use NOW

Here you can find some of the popular tools of today. Remember always check if the one you choose is the last version available and if it covers the need you are looking for. Most of them have free trials you can try before paying the subscription:

A. Natural Language Processing (NLP) Tools

1) **OpenAI GPT-4**: Advanced language model for generating human-like text and conversational AI.

2) **Google BERT**: NLP model for understanding the context of words in search queries.

3) **IBM Watson Natural Language Understanding**: Analyzes text for sentiment, emotion, and keywords.

4) **Microsoft Azure Text Analytics**: Extracts insights such as sentiment and key phrases from text.

5) **Hugging Face Transformers**: Library for building and deploying state-of-the-art NLP models.

B. Machine Learning Platforms

6) **TensorFlow**: Open-source library for building machine learning models with flexible architecture.

7) **PyTorch**: Deep learning framework that offers dynamic computation graphs for flexibility.

8) **Scikit-learn**: Simple and efficient tools for data mining and machine learning in Python.

9) **RapidMiner**: Data science platform for preparing data, creating models, and validating results.

10) **H2O.ai**: Open-source platform for building machine learning models with autoML capabilities.

C. Computer Vision Tools

11) **OpenCV**: Open-source computer vision library for real-time image processing.

12) **Google Cloud Vision**: API for image analysis, including label detection and OCR.

13) **Amazon Rekognition**: Image and video analysis service for detecting objects and faces.

14) **Clarifai**: AI platform for image and video recognition with customizable models.

15) **DeepAI Image Recognition**: AI tool for identifying objects and features in images.

D. Chatbots and Virtual Assistants

16) **Dialogflow**: Google's chatbot development platform for creating conversational interfaces.

17) **Microsoft Bot Framework**: Framework for building and connecting intelligent bots.

18) **ChatGPT**: Conversational AI model for creating interactive chatbots and virtual assistants.

19) **Tidio**: Live chat and chatbot tool for enhancing customer service on websites.

20) **ManyChat**: Chatbot platform focused on automating marketing on Facebook Messenger.

E. Data Analytics and Visualization

21) **Tableau**: Data visualization tool that helps in creating interactive and shareable dashboards.

22) **Power BI**: Microsoft's analytics service for visualizing data and sharing insights.

23) **Looker**: Business intelligence tool for visualizing and analyzing data in real-time.

24) **Qlik Sense**: Data analytics platform that allows users to create interactive reports and dashboards.

25) **Domo**: Cloud-based business intelligence platform for real-time data visualization.

F. Marketing Automation

26) **HubSpot**: Inbound marketing platform that automates email marketing and lead generation.

27) **Marketo**: Marketing automation software for managing campaigns and customer engagement.

28) **Mailchimp**: Email marketing tool with automation features for targeted campaigns.

29) **ActiveCampaign**: Customer experience automation platform for email marketing and CRM.

30) **Drift**: Conversational marketing tool that uses chatbots to engage website visitors.

G. Content Creation and Curation

31) **Copy.ai**: AI-powered tool for generating marketing copies and content ideas.

32) **Jasper**: AI writing assistant that helps create blog posts, social media content, and more.

33) **Writesonic**: AI writing tool for generating high-quality content quickly.

34) **Articoolo**: AI content generator that creates articles based on user-defined topics.

35) **Wordtune**: AI writing assistant that suggests rephrasing and improvements for clarity.

H. Speech Recognition and Synthesis

36) **Google Speech-to-Text**: Converts audio into text using machine learning models.

37) **Amazon Transcribe**: Automatic speech recognition service for transcribing audio files.

38) **IBM Watson Speech to Text**: Converts audio voice into written text for various applications.

39) **Microsoft Azure Speech Service**: Offers speech recognition and synthesis capabilities.

40) **Descript**: Audio and video editing tool with transcription and voice synthesis features.

I. Personalization and Recommendation Systems

41) **Amazon Personalize**: Machine learning service for building personalized product recommendations.

42) **Google Recommendations AI**: Tool for creating tailored product recommendations for users.

43) **Dynamic Yield**: Personalization platform that optimizes customer experiences across channels.

44) **Algolia**: Search and discovery API for building personalized search experiences.

45) **Bloomreach**: Digital experience platform that leverages AI for personalized content delivery.

J. Robotics and Automation

46) **UiPath**: Robotic process automation (RPA) tool for automating repetitive tasks.

47) **Blue Prism**: RPA software for automating business processes and workflows.

48) **Automation Anywhere**: RPA platform that combines traditional automation with AI capabilities.

49) **KUKA Robotics**: Industrial robots and automation solutions for manufacturing.

50) **RPA Express**: Free RPA tool for automating tasks without coding.

K. AI for Financial Services

51) **ZestFinance**: AI-driven credit scoring platform for assessing loan applications.

52) **Kabbage:** AI-powered platform for small business loans and financial insights.

53) **Upstart:** AI lending platform that uses machine learning to assess creditworthiness.

54) **Plaid:** Financial technology platform that connects applications to users' bank accounts.

55) **Kensho:** Analytics and data visualization tools for financial services using AI.

L. AI for Healthcare

56) **IBM Watson Health:** AI solutions for healthcare data analysis and patient insights.

57) **Google Health:** AI tools for improving healthcare outcomes and diagnostics.

58) **Tempus:** Data-driven precision medicine company using AI for cancer treatment insights.

59) **Zebra Medical Vision**: AI radiology solutions for analyzing medical imaging data.

60) **Aidoc:** AI-powered radiology solutions that assist in detecting abnormalities in scans.

M. AI for Human Resources

61) **HireVue:** AI-driven platform for video interviewing and candidate assessment.

62) **Pymetrics:** Uses neuroscience and AI to match candidates with suitable roles.

63) **Breezy HR:** Recruitment software that utilizes AI for sourcing and screening candidates.

64) **Eightfold.ai:** AI talent intelligence platform for recruiting and workforce planning.

65) **XOPA AI:** AI recruitment platform that enhances hiring decisions with data insights.

N. AI for Customer Support

66) **Zendesk:** Customer service platform that integrates AI for ticketing and support.

67) **Freshdesk:** Customer support software that uses AI to automate responses and routing.

68) **Intercom:** Customer messaging platform that leverages AI for personalized support.

69) **Ada:** AI chatbot platform for automating customer support interactions.

70) **LivePerson:** Conversational AI platform for engaging customers through messaging.

O. AI for Project Management

71) **Trello:** Project management tool with AI features for task automation and insights.

72) **Monday.com:** Work operating system that uses AI to optimize project workflows.

73) **Asana:** Project management tool with AI capabilities for task prioritization.

74) **ClickUp:** Productivity platform that leverages AI for project tracking and management.

75) **Wrike:** Collaborative work management software with AI-driven insights and automation.

P. AI for Security

76) **Darktrace:** AI cybersecurity platform that detects and responds to threats in real-time.

77) **CrowdStrike:** Endpoint protection platform that uses AI to prevent cyber threats.

78) **Cylance:** AI-powered antivirus software that predicts and prevents malware attacks.

79) **Snyk:** Security platform that uses AI to identify vulnerabilities in code and dependencies.

80) **Fortinet:** Cybersecurity solutions that leverage AI for threat detection and response.

Q. AI for Supply Chain Management

81) **Llamasoft:** Supply chain analytics platform that uses AI for optimization and simulation.

82) **ClearMetal:** AI-driven supply chain visibility platform for demand forecasting.

83) **Project44:** Logistics platform that provides real-time visibility using AI.

84) **BlueYonder:** AI solutions for supply chain planning and inventory optimization.

85) **Kinaxis:** Supply chain management software that uses AI for rapid decision-making.

R. AI for Security

86) **Darktrace:** AI cybersecurity platform that detects and responds to threats in real-time.

87) **CrowdStrike:** Endpoint protection platform that uses AI to prevent cyber threats.

88) **Cylance:** AI-powered antivirus software that predicts and prevents malware attacks.

89) **Snyk:** Security platform that uses AI to identify vulnerabilities in code and dependencies.

90) **Fortinet:** Cybersecurity solutions that leverage AI for threat detection and response.

S. AI for Education

91) **Knewton:** Adaptive learning technology that personalizes educational content using AI.

92) **Duolingo:** Language-learning platform that uses AI to tailor lessons to user progress.

93) **Socratic by Google:** AI-powered app that helps students with homework and explanations.

94) **Edmodo:** Educational platform that uses AI for personalized learning experiences.

95) **Coursera:** Online learning platform that leverages AI for course recommendations.

T. AI for Creative Arts

96) **DeepArt:** AI tool that transforms photos into artistic styles using neural networks.

97) **Runway ML:** Creative toolkit for artists to use AI in their projects and artwork.

98) **DALL-E:** AI model that generates images from textual descriptions.

99) **Artbreeder:** Collaborative platform for creating and modifying images using AI.

100) **AIVA:** AI composer that creates original music based on user preferences.

www.ingramcontent.com/pod-product-compliance
Lightning Source LLC
Chambersburg PA
CBHW031440210526
45464CB00005B/2278